sew your own
dolls

25 STYLISH DOLLS
TO **MAKE** *AND*
PERSONALIZE

Louise Kelly

CICO BOOKS
LONDON NEW YORK

Published in 2017 by CICO Books
An imprint of Ryland Peters & Small Ltd
20–21 Jockey's Fields   341 E 116th St
London WC1R 4BW   New York, NY 10029

www.rylandpeters.com

10 9 8 7 6 5 4 3

Text © Louise Kelly 2017
Design, illustration, and photography © CICO Books 2017

A CIP catalog record for this book is available from the Library of Congress and the British Library.

ISBN: 978 1 78249 424 9

Printed in China

Editor: Clare Sayer
Designer: Mark Latter
Photographer: Geoff Dann
Stylist: Trina Dalziel
Illustrator: Cathy Brear

In-house editor: Anna Galkina
Art director: Sally Powell
Production controller: David Hearn
Publishing manager: Penny Craig
Publisher: Cindy Richards

contents

CHAPTER ONE 18
vintage & colorful

CHAPTER THREE 84
trendy & hip

CHAPTER TWO 54
cool & cute

introduction

My earliest memory of needle crafting was learning to knit with my Granny Nancy. She was an amazing knitter and seamstress and she could crochet practically anything. Watching her when I was little, I was sure she was magical. In fact, both my grandmothers were of that generation where women were all expert bakers, quilters, knitters, and dressmakers. My sewing journey starts with these two women; I guess, in some ways, they are in everything I make.

My Dad is an amazingly talented artist, so I grew up in an environment where creativity was always encouraged. There seemed to me to be endless amounts of paper at my disposal and strange drawing tools to explore. Dad has never been too precious about his paints and brushes, so I could freely use them, and was never told off for spilling paint or getting messy. Dad's influence on me and my career choice is huge, and is the very reason that I find myself sitting here, writing the introduction to my very first book!

I did learn some embroidery at school—memories of a disastrous embroidered cat cushion that I didn't put much effort in to, and my teacher's comments of disappointment will forever haunt me! Apart from a bit of sewing in my home economics classes, I spent my teenage years aspiring to be a serious artist. Fast forward a few years (ok, quite a few years) and I am teaching kids sewing classes every Saturday morning in the pretty little quilt shop where I used to work. A simple request from a few little girls about a dollmaking class had me researching techniques and making samples, and that was it! My head was suddenly full of little characters and outfits and themes, and once I had started, I couldn't stop. I guess I had found my "thing."

I just love the whole dollmaking process, but perhaps my favorite part is picking out all the pattern pieces that I think I will need, choosing a hairstyle and some shoes, and maybe a bag or a flower for her hair. Before I start stitching I draw around and cut out everything I will need for the doll body, with some music or a movie on. I find this part so relaxing and contemplative. I'm usually thinking about the character of the doll and forming her personality and outfit in my head as I go—and then I bring her to life!

I really do hope that you enjoy this book and get to creating some little dolls and maybe a whole wardrobe of clothes and accessories. Set your creativity free and stitch to your heart's content!

My final piece of advice? Don't get caught up in perfection! Crafting of any sort is intended to be enjoyable, relaxing, and comforting, so don't sweat it if every little thing isn't absolutely perfect, especially when you start making dolls for the first time. By all means unpick your stitches or restart something—but in all honesty, a wonky hairstyle or an off-center pout will only add character and personality. The more dolls you make, the more confident you will become and your own style will develop.

There is just something so wonderful, magical even about making dolls and miniature little things… enjoy it!

the basics

materials

Good-quality materials are essential: not only do they give you a great finished doll, but they are also a pleasure to work with. Sewing is undoubtedly a very tactile endeavor, so lovely fabrics and textures make it really worthwhile and enjoyable.

felt

I could easily chat for hours about felt! However, the key thing to mention is that you need to use good-quality felt. This doesn't necessary mean expensive; there are many beautiful felts out there for great prices. Ideally you should use a 100 percent wool felt, or a wool mix felt that has at least 30 percent wool. Wool felt used to be very coarse and thick, but these days you can find sturdy yet smooth, soft, and fine felt in a vast array of colors. Avoid 100 percent acrylic felt; it won't hold up to a lot of stitching, can become misshapen when stuffed, you can't iron it (it will melt), and it can be squeaky when working with it. It can also pile or get bobbly and certainly won't make your doll last any longer.

stuffing

Toy stuffing is widely available, from craft stores and online. I have yet to come across one that didn't work. Buy a big bag and it will last for ages.

thread

Just as the right needles are important, so too is the right thread. I mostly use six-stranded embroidery floss (cotton) and almost always use just one strand of it, so I cut a length and separate off one strand each time I need a length of thread. You could also use a spool of cotton or polyester thread, which I sometime use for skin tones. Whichever you use, one fine strand and a small needle will be delicate enough for sewing small pieces of felt and cotton.

Embroidery floss (thread) is fairly inexpensive, but it is always best to choose one that is good quality; I know from experience that cheap floss is terrible to work with, as it tangles and breaks easily. See the suppliers on page 126 for my favorite brands. I think of my thread collection like a painter's palette. I keep them in a thread organizer box, wound onto little card bobbins and grouped together in color families, so that I can clearly see all the shades at a glance—I can also tell if I need to replenish the cool grays, yellow greens, or lipstick colors!

cotton fabric

I prefer to use good-quality cotton fabric to make the dolls' clothes—especially pretty vintage prints! I tend to source my fabrics from patchwork and quilting stores or online suppliers, where you can buy fat quarters (bundles of pre-cut fabric, taken from one yard of fabric cut into four pieces) in a wide range of "themes" and colors. You could easily get three or four dresses from one fat quarter!

building your stash

You may already have a collection of fabric to hand and, if you do, I bet you could just dive right in and get started. If you don't already have a stash, here are a few tips on how I build mine.

- Begin by picking the colors and patterns that you like. These will be your feature fabrics. This may seem obvious, but you are the one that will be using them so they should make your heart sing! Don't like florals? Then choose some geometrics or novelty prints. Don't like bright pastel color schemes? Then go for autumnal or primary colors. Pick what you fancy! My feature fabrics are usually florals and often Liberty of London prints—they produce such wonderful tiny florals.

- Once you have your feature fabrics you need to source your "basics." For me these are polka dot and striped fabrics and, of course, solid-color cottons. I like to keep a good stock of these in a variety of colors. I use them for doll pants, a blouse to match a flowery skirt, or a contrasting bodice. Keep your feature fabrics in mind when buying, so that you can mix and match fabrics that complement each other.

- Now keep your eye out for other fabrics to add to your stash: soft cotton-mix denims, lace, tulle, jersey knit, faux suede, and glitter fabrics.

All you need are a few feature prints that really speak to you, a few polka dots and stripes that match, some skin tone and hair-colored felt, a few felt colors for shoes and hair flowers, maybe a fat quarter of denim and instantly, you have a capsule wardrobe ready to sew for your doll!

tools

needles

The wrong needle can ruin your project and the right one will make your sewing a breeze. I favor fine needles; in fact, I almost exclusively use size 10 Sharps. For me they are perfect for sewing small things. If you use a needle that is too big or thick, it could disrupt or tear the edge of your felt, for example, and the seams won't hold up to stuffing. You will also need a doll needle or a long embroidery needle for attaching limbs.

glue pen

My fabric glue pen is the most favored and trusted tool in my kit! Although I do use pins occasionally, more often than not the pattern pieces that I work with are too small to take a pin. This is where the glue pen comes in; I use it to secure small hems and seam allowances, keep eyes in place while their lashes are being stitched, hold hair in place while I add curls and waves, and for a multitude of other little bits and pieces. It dries clear (except on very dark fabrics, where it will dry white-ish,) it's very easy to sew through, and it doesn't gum up your needle. It's also washable and non-permanent. I use a Sewline fabric glue pen, as they can be refilled easily.

pins

For the same reasons that I choose fine needles, I always use fine pins—they slip through the fabric and felt without tearing or leaving "puncture marks."

fabric pens, markers and pencils

I have tried many different fabric marking tools over the years; some can be removed with water while some are air-erasable and you can even use felt tips, rollerballs, pencils, or discs of chalk. Some even come with their own erasing fluid! But by far my most favored fabric marking tools are the ones with thermo-sensitive inks (in other words, heat erasable). The ink in these pens becomes transparent with friction or heat.

Traditionally, these are used by quilters to mark seams on their patchwork projects—the ink is then removed with an iron. I use them for drawing around templates, adding seam allowances, and sketching faces and hair texture directly onto the felt and I use a hairdryer to remove the marks when I'm finished!

Making marks on dark fabrics requires a different tool —I love the Sewline Fabric Pencil, which works just like a regular mechanical pencil, except that it uses ingenious ceramic leads (I especially like the white or pink leads). You can get much more accurate marks with it as opposed to tailor's chalk or a fabric chalk pencil.

haemostats

This little tool changed my dollmaking! Haemostats help you to push the stuffing into the nooks and crannies of the pattern pieces without having to squish or crumple your fabric, which is especially useful for limbs and hair. They allow you to vary the firmness of the stuffing, too. They are also incredibly useful when it comes to turning bodies, limbs, and heads the right way out after stitching. Essentially they look like a long pair of tongs, a little like a piece of medical equipment. You can buy haemostats for crafting from most good stores in a range of sizes. I recommend the 6 in. (15 cm) or 8 in. (20 cm) ones. The alternative is to use the end of a pencil to push stuffing into limbs, although you won't get as much control.

scissors

Who doesn't love a beautiful pair of scissors? Here's what you need to see you through all your dollmaking projects:

• A small pair of embroidery scissors—perfect for snipping threads and cutting small pattern pieces.

• A larger pair of fabric shears—for cutting larger pattern pieces and general fabric use.

• A pair of pinking shears, which are great for cutting cotton or other fabric that may fray, and for creating decorative edges

• I also have an inexpensive pair of scallop-edge scissors— again for creating decorative edges quickly.

Scissors can range in price from cheap to astronomical but, as with most crafting tools, it's a good idea to invest in a really good pair of fabric scissors: if you look after them well, they will last you a lifetime. Never EVER let anyone use your fabric scissors for cutting paper or wire or anything other than fabric and thread!

other miscellaneous items

I always have a small 6 in. (15 cm) quilter's ruler within arm's reach when I'm working—I use it to add seam allowances and check measurements, because it gives really accurate results.

I also really enjoy using a tear-away stabilizer. It's incredibly useful when you are embroidering on fabrics that are delicate or flimsy. I use it when stitching the features on my doll faces, especially the lashes and lips. It basically adds structure to the fabric and really holds the stitches in place. When you're done, you just tear away the excess!

And last, but not least, some cardstock for cutting out templates and a pair of papercutting scissors—don't ever use your fabric scissors!

techniques

using templates

All my designs begin as sketches, which then become individual shapes for all the different components, and then I draft a final pattern piece with nice clean lines and straight edges. You'll find all of these in the templates section at the back of the book. All the dolls (with the exception of one or two) are made in the same way, so you'll use the same templates for the Basic Doll over and again, as well as some of the accessories pattern pieces.

So my advice for you is to enlarge the templates from the back of the book (you can use a photocopier for this) as you need them (no need to do them all at once) and then trace them onto card (or use your photocopies). Cut them out and keep them in a file or box, always ready at hand for you to reuse! I keep mine in a little expandable file, with compartments for body parts, hairstyles, clothes, shoes, and accessories so that I can always find what I need.

For the larger and smaller dolls, the templates can be enlarged or reduced (see Heidi and Maisie on pages 104 and 67). Many of the templates include stitching lines and seam allowance guides, so refer back to the template section where necessary.

handstitching doll bodies

All the dolls in this book are handstitched. I use a small backstitch, working just a few millimeters from the edge of the fabric, to put the bodies together. Small, regular stitches are ideal but don't worry about making them absolutely perfect—the most important thing is to create nice clean lines and strong seams that will withstand firm stuffing. Backstitch is especially helpful for creating curved seams.

I find it helpful to first tie a knot in your thread, as you normally would, but instead of tying a knot when you finish that length of thread, or line or stitching, which can be cumbersome, just weave your needle and thread through the back of a few stitches and snip the excess thread. At each turning gap and when sewing around the perimeter of the body, overstitch or take a few stitches on top of each other to really strengthen the stitches.

stuffing

It took me a while to really realize how important the stuffing process is to your finished doll and even the character of your doll—it's almost like sculpting! Here are my tips:

- Pull out a huge handful of stuffing onto your work surface, then nip off smaller handfuls depending on what you are filling. Gently tease this small ball of stuffing into a strip or a "sausage" shape; this will make it much easier to work with and gives a far better finish than trying to force a ball of stuffing into a small turning gap.

- Using the haemostats, push the stuffing to the furthest part of the piece—for example, the feet or hands for the limbs.

- When stuffing limbs, stuff the feet/hand area quite firmly, continuing along the length and then stuffing a little less firmly at the top. When you add in the strip of stuffing, push or tamp down the first part and feed the rest in, leaving the end quite loose and even poking out of the turning gap; then add the next strip of stuffing to it. This means that each strip will blend seamlessly into the next and you won't get lumps and bumps. (Note that the arms are attached with the closed turning gap at the back and to the top, so it won't be seen on your finished doll.)

- When stuffing the body and the head, first give a light, even stuffing of the whole shape, using the same strip method but without tamping down. Then pay attention to the neck and any curves of the hair; I use smaller pieces of stuffing to fill these areas fairly firmly, especially the neck and shoulder area. It's helpful to roll a small piece of stuffing and use the haemostats to place it exactly where you want it. Move evenly around the body, filling it until it is quite firm; work around the top of the head filling the shape of the hair firmly, also—but it should be a softer fill around the neck opening. If you find that the seam around the top of the head is puckered, gently push into it with the stuffing and haemostats until you get the desired shape.

hand stitches

Embroidery is a wonderful craft to explore and there are literally hundreds of variations of stitches for you to explore. Here are some of the most common hand stitches, and the ones that are used throughout this book.

running stitch

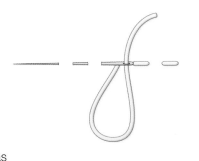

This is a basic stitch that has many applications. It creates a broken or dashed line, and is both functional and decorative. Slight variations are known as basting (tacking) stitch, which are longer running stitches used to temporarily hold layers of fabric together while they are sewn with a smaller, more regular stitch—the basting stitches are them removed. Mostly used here for sewing the waistline of doll pants and for basting. Simply bring the needle up and back down through the fabric, keeping the spaces between the stitches the same size as the stitches themselves.

whip stitch

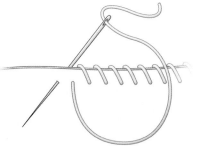

This is a decorative and functional overcast stitch. It is a very quick way of sealing the edges of two or more layers of fabric. In this book it is mostly used for attaching tiny felt collars, adding hoods to coats, and making doll boots. Push the needle through the first layer of fabric, starting "inside" the seam. Next, take the needle over the seam and push through both layers of fabric, so that the needle comes through in the same position. Repeat, pushing the needle through the same hole as before—but this time angle the needle so that it comes out a short distance from the first stitch. Continue to make a series of "parallel" stitches.

backstitch

The most widely used stitch throughout the book. It is both decorative and functional, and it creates a continuous line of stitches, which is perfect for seams and hems and also for adding detail to hair and around the eyes. Bring the needle up from the back, one stitch length to the left of your "start" point. Insert it one stitch length to the right and then bring it up again one stitch length in front of the point where the needle first emerged. Always work back into where the last stitch ended; this will give you a nice unbroken line.

blanket stitch

This stitch is both decorative and functional and is often used in appliqué and for sealing the edges of fabric. Throughout the book it is used to attach eyes and along the edges of coats. Bring the needle through at the edge of the fabric. Push the needle back through the fabric a short distance from the edge and loop the thread under the needle. Pull the thread through to make the first stitch, then make another stitch to the right of this. Continue along the fabric.

satin stitch

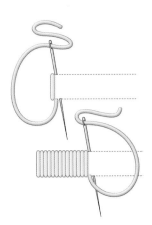

Satin stitch is a decorative filler stitch. It consists of a series of straight stitches laid close together to completely fill a shape without any gaps. It is used throughout the book for sewing doll lips. See page 14, step 6, for more tips on stitching tiny mouths.

ladder stitch

Ladder stitch is a functional and very handy stitch to know. It is used to seamlessly close the turning gaps on doll bodies and limbs after stuffing. It can also be used to repair a tear or an uneven seam! Neatly fold the seams before you start. Catch the first edge with your needle and take a very small stitch. Cross to the other side and pick up a tiny stitch on the fold, then return to the other side, again picking up a stitch on the fold. Work a few stitches before pulling closed and then continue along the gap.

french knot

A purely decorative stitch and very versatile, a knot is created on the surface of your work by wrapping the thread around the needle. Various sizes can be achieved by using different threads and more or fewer wraps. Keeping the wraps on the needle neat (but not tight) will result in a lovely French knot. I use them for highlights on the doll's eyes. They are also useful for adding dots and small circles to build texture.

making the basic doll

All the dolls in this book are made using the same basic pattern to create a doll that is approximately 13 in. (33 cm) tall. Templates for all the pattern pieces are given on pages 110–115; some of these are actual size, but some of them will need to be enlarged by the percentage given. If you want to make a doll that is smaller or larger, simply increase or reduce all the pattern pieces by the same amount and adjust the fabric amounts accordingly.

Cut out all the doll body pieces from skin-tone felt and the two eye pieces from black felt. There are 12 different hairstyles to choose from, so select which one you want to use and cut this from felt also.

body and limbs

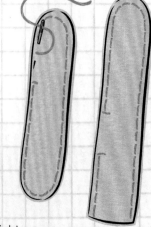

1 Begin by sewing the limbs. For the arms, place two arm pieces together and backstitch all around, leaving a turning gap of approximately ½ in. (1 cm) on a straight edge. For the legs, sew all the way around in the same manner but leave the top open.

2 Turn each limb out the right way. Haemostats are a great tool for turning arms and legs, or you could use the rounded end of a pen or the wrong end of a knitting needle.

3 For the body, place the two body back pieces together and, using a ¼-in. (5-mm) seam allowance, backstitch together, leaving a turning gap of around ¾ in. (2 cm) in the lower portion of the body.

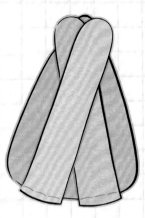

4 Next attach the legs to the body front, using just a few basting (tacking) stitches to hold them in place. These stitches won't be seen when the body is finished.

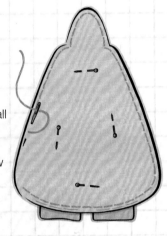

5 Now place the back and front sections right sides together so that the legs are in between the two pieces. Backstitch all around the edge. You may have to fold the legs down—a few well-placed pins will keep the legs in place while you sew around the body.

6 Turn out the right way by pulling the legs and then the rest of the body out through the turning gap that you left in the back. Run your haemostats or the wrong end of the knitting needle around the seams to get a nice clean shape.

face and hair

1 Place the front section of your chosen hairstyle over the head piece, secure with a glue pen, and then backstitch all around the hairline to secure the two pieces together. Add any extra lines of stitching for curls, waves, or flicks.

2 Next sew the back section of the hair onto the neck. Use the front face and hair piece as a guide for positioning and stitch 1 in. (2.5 cm) or so at the base of the neck.

3 Lightly sketch the face with a washable fabric pen. Use the eye template to draw around and add in a few eyelashes. Add a small dash for the nose and the lips directly below. Draw the lips by making a curved line for the center on the mouth, then add the top lip, then the bottom lip.

4 Take the two eye pieces and fix them in place with the glue pen. Then stitch all around the eyes using a blanket stitch and black embroidery floss (cotton). Now you can add the detail around the eye: using a backstitch, begin with the curved line at the inner part of the eye, stitching up over the top of the eye and out to the lashes—just how you would apply eyeliner! Once you have stitched the basic eyeliner shape, you can add some definition to the lashes by going back and forth with some freeform stitches to thicken them at the base. One or two French knots in white embroidery floss (cotton) will add some sweet highlights to your doll's eyes and bring them to life!

5 Make one or two tiny stitches for the nose, using a thread that is just a few shades darker than your doll's skin tone.

6 To sew the mouth, begin by "lining" the lips with your choice of lipstick-colored thread in backstitch. This will act as a guide when filling the lips in with satin stitch. Start at the center of the top lip, work out to the side, then return back to the center and work out toward the other side of the mouth. Be sure to place your needle on the outside of your guideline, as this will help give a nice clean line to the lip shape. Repeat for the bottom lip. Make your stitches diagonal to give the lips some depth; you can always go back over and perfect the shape.

7 Place the front and back head pieces right sides together and backstitch all around, leaving a 1 in. (2.5 cm) turning gap at the chin. Use an extra seam allowance for ponytails and buns, then snip into these seam allowances to give a nice, clean, curved line. Turn the head out the right way and fold in the neck

stuffing the doll

1 Stuff the legs, arms, and body through the turning gaps until fairly stiff. When stuffing the head, take small pieces to first fill out any buns, ponytails, or bumps, then use the filling to shape the rest of the head. Be careful not to over stuff the head to avoid it becoming too heavy, but stuff it enough so that it has a clean shape with no puckering around the seam.

2 Close all gaps using a ladder stitch.

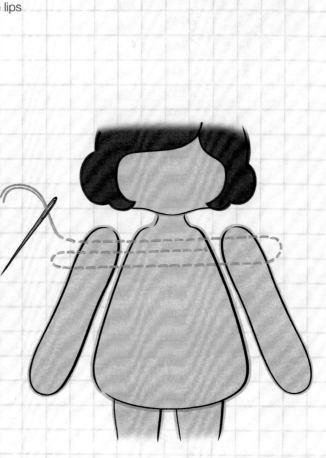

assembly

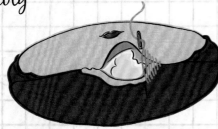

1 Begin by using a ladder stitch to "lessen" the gap at the chin to ensure that the neck fits snugly. Close evenly on either side using a ladder stitch, checking as you go that the head fits nicely onto the neck. Line the neck up directly under the lips for good placement.

2 Place the head on the neck and secure all the way around using a ladder stitch. Use a few pins to hold the head steady while you do this.

3 To attach the arms, you will need a doll needle (or any other long sewing needle). Use double thread and start by passing the thread through the shoulders a few times until the thread feels secure. Now add the arms; you will be sewing through an arm, the shoulders, and then the other arm, back and forth until the arms are very secure. Finish by adding a ¼-in. (6-mm) button to each arm; these will keep the arms in position and stop them from loosening over time.

doll pants

1 Cut two doll pants pieces from cotton fabric.

2 To make a name tag, write your doll's name on some white or cream felt and embroider over the lines using a backstitch. Sketch an oval or rounded square shape around the name and cut it out; you can then place the name tag on a coordinating piece of felt and cut around using pinking shears or scalloped scissors. Use a glue pen to secure the two felt pieces together and then attach the name tag to the center of one of your doll pants pieces by stitching around the embroidered name in running stitch.

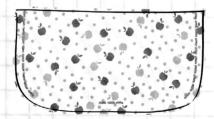

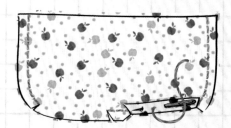

3 Using the doll pants template as a guide, sketch some sewing guides onto the wrong side of one of the pattern pieces using a washable fabric pen. First sew the gusset (this will only take a few stitches), then sew down either side of the doll pants.

4 To finish the leg holes, make small diagonal snips into the fabric where the stitching starts and ends and then turn a hem to the wrong side. Sew around each leg hole, use a running stitch or backstitch.

5 Turn down a ¼-in. (5-mm) seam at the waistline and place some fine elastic in it. Stitch all around using a running stitch or backstitch. Be careful not to catch the elastic with your needle or to sew through it. Before you finish sewing around the waist, try the pants on your doll for fit, pull the elastic to gather the waist, and tie in a double knot. Remove the pants, trim the elastic, and finish sewing the hem closed.

shoe

1 Cut out the shoe pattern pieces, from either felt, glitter fabric, or faux suede. You will need two uppers and two soles.

2 Sew around the opening in the front to add strength and structure. (Skip this step if you are using glitter fabric or if you are making boots that have no shape cut out from the front.)

3 Place the shoe upper and shoe sole right sides together and stitch together, leaving the top open. Turn out the right way. Stitch around the top if you are using felt and it feels as if it needs some strengthening. Repeat to make a second shoe.

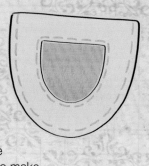

basic bodice

These bodice instructions are invaluable, as they form the basis of almost all of the outfits in the book. Dresses, crop tops, sweaters, and blouses—are all variations of this pattern!

1 Use the templates on page 112 to cut out the front and back bodice pieces (note that all seam allowances are included in the template). As you will be using these templates over and again, it's a good idea to copy them onto some cardstock; you can then easily drawn around them with a washable fabric pen.

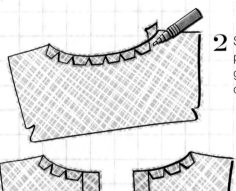

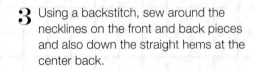

2 Snip into the curve of the neckline on all the bodice pieces, turn it over to the wrong side, and secure with a glue pen. Also turn over the small hem at the center back of each back bodice piece.

3 Using a backstitch, sew around the necklines on the front and back pieces and also down the straight hems at the center back.

4 Place the front bodice and one back bodice right sides together and backstitch together at the shoulder. Repeat for the other back bodice piece.

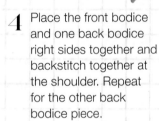

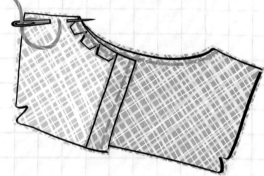

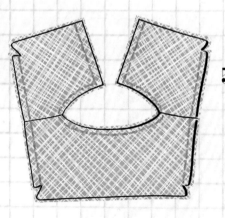

5 Open out the bodice, turn in a small hem at the sleeves, and secure with the glue pen. Sew both sleeve hems, using a backstitch or running stitch.

6 Without cutting your thread, place the bodice right sides together again and sew from the underarm to the waistline. Repeat for the other side and the bodice is finished, all ready for you to attach a skirt, make a dress, or finish with a hem to make a top or blouse!

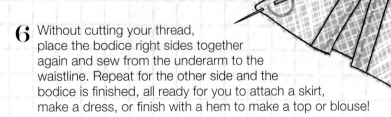

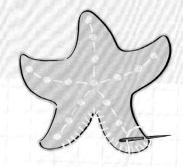

vintage & colorful

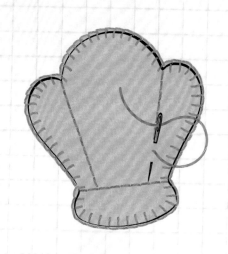

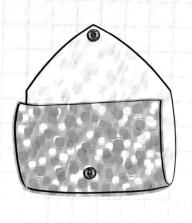

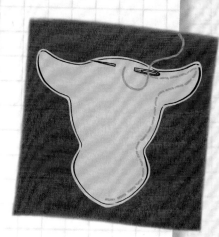

amber

Amber has everything she needs for a slumber party with her friends. Her cami-top and shorts pajama set is trimmed with adorable mini pom-poms. She even has her own monogrammed wool blanket to snuggle under. And those cute slippers? Every girl needs a pair of bunny slippers!

you will need

Basic doll templates on page 110

Wavy hair template on page 119

Amber templates on page 112

Skin-tone and black felt for the doll

Stranded embroidery floss (cotton) in assorted colors

Two coordinating fabrics for the cami-top, shorts, and yoke

Small pieces of felt for the name tag

Small length of fine elastic

20 in. (50 cm) mini pom-pom trim

One ⅛-in. (4-mm) buttons

Two snap fasteners

Small pieces of white and pink felt for the slippers

10 x 12 in. (25 x 30 cm) wool fabric for the blanket (I used a remnant of an old woollen blanket, but you could also use felt, fleece, flannel etc.)

Glue pen

Basic sewing kit

cutting out and making the doll

Using the templates for the Basic Doll and the Wavy hair, cut out, stitch, and assemble the doll, following the instructions on page 12.

cami-top

1 Using the templates on page 112, cut one cami-top front and two cami-top backs from one of your fabrics.

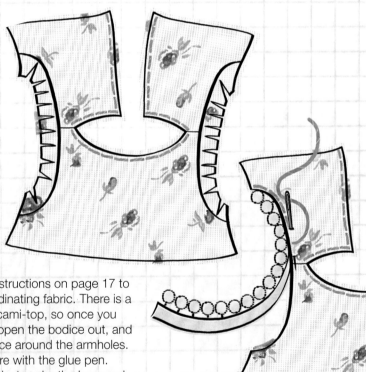

2 Follow steps 2–4 of the basic bodice instructions on page 17 to make the cami-top from the other coordinating fabric. There is a slightly different armhole shape for the cami-top, so once you have joined the front and back pieces, open the bodice out, and then snip into the curved seam allowance around the armholes. Turn a hem to the wrong side and secure with the glue pen. Position a length of mini pom-pom trim just under the hem and stitch in place using backstitch. Complete the bodice by turning right sides together and stitching from the underarm to the waistband (see step 6 of basic bodice, page 17).

Tip: I always cut any trim after I have finished stitching it on—that way I avoid wastage.

3 For the skirt portion of the cami-top, cut a strip from the same fabric that is 2 x 13 in. (5 x 33 cm). First fold and glue a small hem at one end of your fabric strip, then place the bodice and fabric strip right sides together, with the waistband of the bodice lined up with the top right-hand edge of the fabric strip. Backstitch along the waistband, with approx. ⅛-in. (3-mm) seam allowance, folding small ¼-in. (5-mm) pleats every two stitches or so as you go. You may not need all 13 in. (33 cm) of this fabric strip—you can just trim off any extra, ensuring that you leave enough to turn a small hem at the end. Of course, you could always cut a longer strip and add more pleats to make a fuller skirt.

4 Cut out the yoke pattern piece from the same fabric as the shorts, using the template on page 112. Snip into the seam allowance and turn in to neaten the edges. Place on the bodice front and stitch around the edge, then add a little ⅛-in. (4-mm) button, too. Add two snap fasteners to the back of the bodice.

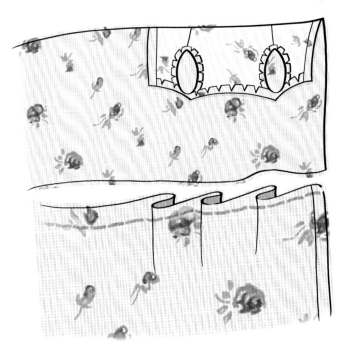

5 Fold under a ¼-in. (5-mm) hem at the bottom of the skirt and add mini pom-pom trim in the same way as you did around the armholes.

shorts

Follow the instructions for the doll pants on page 16, cutting them from your other coordinating fabric. Add some mini pom-pom trim around the bottom of the legs.

bunny slippers

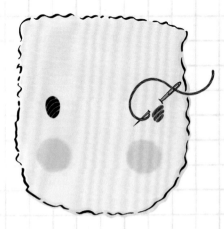

1 Using the templates on page 112, cut four pink soles, two white uppers, two white outer ears, and two pink inner ears. (Note that each slipper has two soles to give strength.)

2 Begin by stitching the bunny faces, using the template as a sewing guide. Stitch two little ovals in backstitch for the eyes and then satin stitch over the top to fill them in. (You could use small pieces of black felt instead and stitch around the edges.) Add a few freeform straight stitches for the pink nose and the mouth. You could use some blush on the bunny cheeks, too. How cute!

3 Take two pink sole pieces and lay a white slipper upper on top. Starting at the center of one side, blanket stitch around the whole slipper shape and then across the top of the upper.

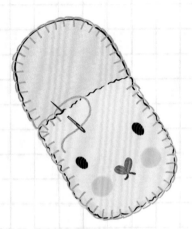

4 Secure the pink inner ears to the white outer ears with glue pen and a few stitches, then add to the main slipper. Pinch or fold the bottom of the bunny ear and secure using a few tiny stitches.

blanket

Take your piece of wool fabric for the blanket and use scissors to round each corner. Blanket stitch all the way around the edge and then embroider the doll's initial in the bottom left-hand corner in backstitch. Once you have stitched the initial outline of the letter, you can go back over it to thicken and neaten the line.

chloe

Chloe is wearing her favorite Christmas sweater for her favorite time of year! With the presents wrapped and the decorations hung, she is all set for some festivities with her loved ones. Her adorable reindeer sweater is made from felt with a reindeer motif on the front-Rudolf's nose even matches Chloe's red glitter shoes!

you will need

Basic doll templates on page 110

Center parting hair template on page 119

Chloe templates on page 114

Skin-tone, brown, and black felt for the doll

Stranded embroidery floss (cotton) in assorted colors

Cotton fabric for the pants

Small length of fine elastic

3½ x 13 in. (9 x 33 cm) denim fabric for the skirt

Navy felt for the sweater

Small piece of tan felt for the reindeer head

Red and gold glitter fabric for the shoes, nose, and antlers

Small pieces of felt for the name tag

Two snap fasteners

Glue pen

Basic sewing kit

cutting out and making the doll

Using the templates for the Basic Doll and the Center Parting hair, cut out, stitch, and assemble the doll, following the instructions on page 12.

doll pants

Follow the instructions for the doll pants on page 16.

skirt

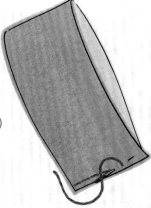

1 Fold the piece of denim fabric in half, wrong sides together and lining up the two short ends. Backstitch with a ¼-in. (5-mm) seam allowance, leaving about ¼ in. (5 mm) unstitched at the top (waist).

2 Fold ¼ in. (5 mm) over to the wrong side at the waist and position the piece of fine elastic inside. Stitch around the waist of the skirt, being careful not to sew through the elastic. Stop about 1 in. (2.5 cm) before you finish and don't cut your thread.

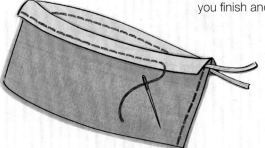

3 Try the skirt on your doll for fit (no need to turn it right side out at this stage) and gently pull the elastic to gather the waist. Tie the elastic in a double knot and trim. Remove the skirt from the doll and finish sewing around the waist, then turn a small ¼-in. (5-mm) hem under at the bottom and stitch in place.

christmas sweater

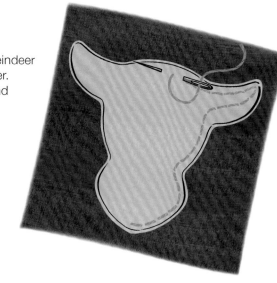

1 Using the templates on page 114, cutting the sweater pieces from navy felt, the reindeer head pieces from tan felt, the nose and shoes from red glitter fabric, and the antlers from gold glitter fabric.

2 Begin by attaching the reindeer to the front of the sweater. Stitch around his face and ears using a backstitch.

3 Stitch some detail on his face; some small black satin stitches or even a French knot will work well for his eyes and some straight stitches for his mouth (which you could add after he gets his nose).

4 Now add his little red nose and gold antlers. Just using the glue pen here is sufficient, but you can take a few discrete stitches around the edge in a matching thread.

5 Place the front of the sweater and one of the back pieces right sides together and sew at the shoulders. Repeat for the second back piece.

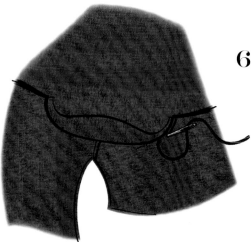

6 Add the sleeves: place the main body of the sweater and one sleeve right sides together. Stitch together about ⅛ in. (3 mm) in from the edge, "easing" the sleeve into position by lining up the edges of the two pieces every few stitches as you sew. Repeat for the other sleeve.

Tip: To make your glitter even more sparkly, you could use a gloss medium, most often used in papercrafting—simply dab onto the nose and antlers before adding to the sweater. It will give them a lovely raised-up shiny look.

7 Once both sleeves have been added, fold so that the front and back are right sides together again and sew up the sleeve from the "cuff" to the underarm and from the underarm down the side of the sweater. Repeat for the other side.

8 Turn out the right way and turn under a hem along both center back straight edges. Add two snap fasteners. Sew a small blanket stitch around the bottom of the sweater and around the neckline. Put the sweater on your doll and turn up the sleeves.

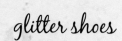

glitter shoes

Use the templates for the Basic Shoe on page 111 to cut out two soles and two uppers from red glitter fabric. Follow the instructions on page 16 to complete the shoes.

elise

Elise has a penchant for anything vintage, including her sense of style. Her outfit is a nod to the elegance and beauty of the 1940s—high-waisted, wide-leg jeans and a ditsy print button-down blouse, topped off with a hair tie to keep her curls and waves in place.

you will need

Basic doll templates on page 110

Side-swept hair template on page 118

Elise templates on page 113

Skin-tone, brown, and black felt for the doll

Stranded embroidery floss (cotton) in assorted colors

Denim fabric for the jeans

Four snap fasteners

Small print cotton fabric for the blouse

Two ⅛-in. (4-mm) buttons

Coordinating fabric for the hair tie

Felt for the shoes

Glue pen

Basic sewing kit

cutting out and making the doll

Using the templates for the Basic Doll and the Side-swept hair, cut out, stitch, and assemble the doll, following the instructions on page 12.

jeans

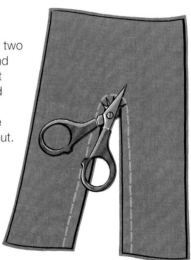

1 Using the template on page 113 cut two jean pieces from the denim fabric and place them right sides together. First backstitch around the inner legs and then make snips around the top of the inner leg seam allowance to give a nice smooth shape when turned out.

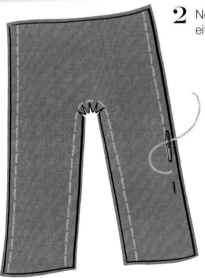

2 Now backstitch down either side of the jeans.

3 To finish the waist you could add some fine elastic to make a gathered waist, as if you were making the doll pants (see page 16), but to give Elise's jeans the high-waist look, I have added two snap fasteners to two folds in the back. Begin by turning down a ¼-in. (5-mm) hem and stitching all around, then try the jeans on your doll for fit. Make two pleats or folds in the back to give a nice smooth shape at the front and a good fit on the waist. Mark these folds with a fabric pen and remove the jeans from the doll. Add a snap fastener to the inside of each fold.

4 Turn the jeans out the right way and make some turn-ups at each leg, folding over twice to hide any raw edges.

v-neck blouse

1 Using the templates on page 113, cut one blouse back and two blouse fronts from print cotton fabric. Follow the instructions on page 17 for the basic bodice, but without snipping into the seam allowance at the neckline. Unlike the basic bodice, the blouse is fastened at the front, so all you need to do is fold in a hem at each side to create the V shape of the neckline (the blouse is technically worn "back to front").

2 Finish the bottom of the blouse with a small hem. Add two snap fasteners down the front and add the buttons for decoration.

hair tie

1 Cut two strips of cotton fabric each 5 x ½ in. (12.5 x 1 cm). Fold each long raw edge in to the center and use the glue pen to secure. Make a diagonal fold at one end of each strip and secure with glue pen (you could also stitch along the length of each strip with backstitch or running stitch, but it is up to you.

2 The hair tie is offset slightly, so trim about ¾ in. (2 cm) from one of the pieces (make sure you don't trim off the diagonal end).

3 Position the strips at each side of the head, so that they are facing toward the back of the head. Stitch them in place along the seams in the hair, then fold the strips in over the front of the head into the right positions—this gives a nice finished edge.

4 Now take the small piece that was trimmed off earlier and wrap it around where the strips cross. Use the glue pen to help hold everything in place, then add a few stitches to secure.

shoes

Use the templates for the Pointy Shoe on page 111 to cut out two soles and two uppers from red felt. Follow the instructions on page 16 to complete the shoes.

ava

Ava thinks there is nothing better than spending a spring afternoon in her delightful garden, tending to all of her beautiful plants. Her long floaty maxi-dress, in a Liberty of London floral print of course, perfectly suits her chilled personality. The pretty rose in her hair came straight from her favorite rose bush!

you will need

Basic doll templates on page 110

Top-knot hair template on page 119

Ava templates on page 113

Skin-tone, brown, and black felt for the doll

Stranded embroidery floss (cotton) in assorted colors

Cotton fabric for the pants

Small length of fine elastic

Cotton fabric for the maxi dress

Red felt for the shoes and rose

Small piece of green felt for the leaf

Small pieces of felt for the name tag

Two snap fasteners

Fine elastic

Glue pen

Basic sewing kit

cutting out and making the doll

Using the templates for the Basic Doll and the Top-knot hair, cut out, stitch, and assemble the doll, following the instructions on page 12. Note that Ava's hair goes over one eye, so you will need to sketch and stitch the eyes before attaching the hair.

doll pants

Follow the instructions for the doll pants on page 16.

dress

1 Using the templates on page 113, cut one bodice front and two bodice backs from cotton fabric. Follow the basic bodice instructions on page 17, but instead of turning a hem at the sleeves, snip into the seam allowance at the armhole, turn under, and stitch.

2 Use the same cotton fabric to cut a strip measuring 7½ x 9½ in. (19 x 24 cm) for the skirt of the dress..

3 Add the skirt to the bodice in the same way as for Olivia's dress on page 96: fold a small hem at either end of the skirt fabric. Place the bodice and the skirt right sides together and stitch across, folding small pleats as you go. However, you need fewer pleats for the maxi dress to give shape to the waist (and for fit) without adding too much volume. This way the dress will drape nicely at the bottom. You should need about six pleats, so it's a good idea to mark the position of the pleats on the bodice before you start.

4 Turn under a ¼ in. (5 mm) hem around the bottom of the dress and sew using backstitch.

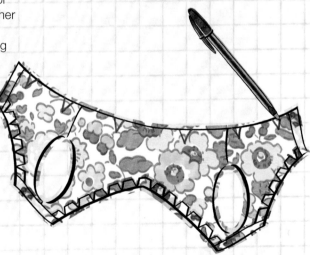

5 Place the two edges of the skirt right sides together and secure with a few pins. Backstitch along the seam, leaving 2 in. (5 cm) at the bottom of the skirt for a split and 2 in. (5 cm) at the top of the skirt (you will only need to stitch for about 3½ in. (9 cm).

6 Turn the dress out the right way. Using backstitch, finish the hems at the split and the opening at the top of the skirt. Add two snap fasteners to the bodice.

Tip: Precision isn't essential to make the rose, so you could just use the template as a guide to sketch the rose shape directly onto the felt using washable fabric pen. Different-sized petals and wavy edges give the rose more realism!

rose

1 Use the templates on page 113 to cut out the large rose from red felt and the leaf from green felt.

2 Starting at either end simply roll the rose up. Keep the bottom flat and once completely rolled, secure will a pin pushed right through the center. Stitch through all the layers so that the rose doesn't unravel. These stitches won't be seen, so the aim here is to secure all the layers. If you think your rose needs an extra few individual petals to round its shape out or to even it up, then just cut out a few semicircles and attach them using a whipstitch.

3 Using a thread to match the hair color, attach the leaf to the underside of the rose with a few random straight stitches (these stitches will be hidden), then, without cutting the thread, attach to the base of the top-knot.

shoes

Use the templates for the Basic Shoe on page XX to cut out two soles and two uppers from red felt. Follow the instructions on page 16 to complete the shoes.

lily

Lily looks effortlessly chic and sophisticated in her navy dress coat, worn over a boat-neck dress that has complementary stripes and peach tones. Subtle hints of pale gold finish everything off. It's simply the perfect ensemble for a fancy lunch with the girls!

cutting out and making the doll

Using the templates for the Basic Doll and the Vintage Waves hair, cut out, stitch, and assemble the doll, following the instructions on page 12.

doll pants

Follow the instructions for the doll pants on page 16.

dress

1 Follow the instructions on page 17 to make the basic bodice from striped fabric.

2 Cut a strip of peach cotton fabric about 3½ x 20 in. (9 x 50 cm) for the skirt part of the dress. You may not need all 20 in. (50 cm) of fabric here; as a rule of thumb, folding a small pleat every two or three stitches will use an average of 13–15 in. (32–38 cm) of fabric. However, you can add more pleats or make them wider to give a fuller look to the dress.

   Tip: Cut a wider or narrower strip of fabric for a longer or shorter skirt!

3 With right side facing up, turn a small hem at the right-hand end of your skirt strip. Place the bodice and the skirt right sides together (the bodice should be on top), lining up both edges at the top right-hand corner. Use a backstitch with a ⅛-in. (3-mm) seam allowance and fold small ¼-in. (5-mm) pleats as you go, perhaps adding two or three stitches between each one. When you get to the far end, turn a small hem and secure with glue pen. Stitch the hem at either end of the skirt and turn a hem along the bottom, sewing with a backstitch.

4 Add two snap fasteners to the back of the bodice and two buttons to cover them.

dress coat

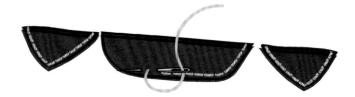

1 Lily's dress coat is put together using the same steps as Olivia's duffle coat on page 98, leaving out the pockets and adding a collar in place of the hood and a few round buttons instead of toggles. Using the Olivia duffle coat templates on page 121, cut one coat back, two coat fronts, and two sleeves from navy felt. Follow steps 2–6 of Olivia's duffle coat on page 98 to make the main body of the coat, turning under a small hem around the bottom of the coat and backstitching to secure.

2 Use the Lily templates on page 120 to cut out all the collar pieces from navy felt. Take the left two collar front pieces and place them together, using the glue pen to fix them in place while you sew. With contrasting peach thread (one strand if using embroidery floss), stitch around the bottom edges using a backstitch. Repeat this process for the right front collar and the back collar, too.

3 Using a matching thread to the coat color, whipstitch the collar pieces in place around the neckline of the coat. Keep your stitches small, but make sure that you sew through all layers of the neckline and collar. Add the three buttons down the left coat front and turn up the sleeves.

clutch bag

1 Using the template on page 120, cut one clutch bag from the gold glitter fabric. If you really want to go to town you could cut another clutch bag pattern piece from cotton (perhaps a scrap from Lily's dress) to use as a lining. There's no need to sew it in place—just use some glue pen to press it to the wrong side of the glitter fabric.

shoes

Use the templates for the Pointy Shoe on page 111 to cut out two soles and two uppers from gold glitter fabric. Follow the instructions on page 16 to complete the shoes.

2 Fold the bag so that the bag flap overlaps the front. Use the haemostats to press the folds in place to create the shape of the bag.

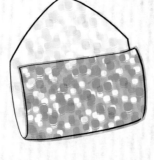

3 Sew the snap fastener in place using a fine needle and strong thread.

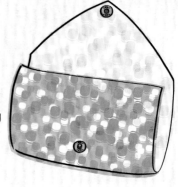

4 Open the bag out again, apply fabric glue to the sides, and fold the bag in place. Press together for a minute or so until the glue holds. Apply a flat-back pearl to the front and leave to dry completely.

mia

Mia plans to spend most of her summer vacations at the beach. She likes to while away the hours collecting shells and listening to the sounds of the sea. Delicate stripes make a lovely print for her two-piece swimsuit. Pick a contrasting color of felt for her flip-flops and bow, then add a sweet little starfish in her hair.

you will need

Basic doll templates on page 110

Vintage waves hair template on page 118

Mia templates on page 122

Skin-tone, brown, and black felt for the doll

Stranded embroidery floss (cotton) in assorted colors

Striped cotton for the swimsuit

Small length of fine elastic

Coral/red felt for the flip-flops and bow

Small pieces of yellow and pink felt for the starfish and shell

Small pieces of felt for the name tag

Small piece of glitter fabric

Piece of fine elastic

Two snap fasteners

Three flat-back pearls

Washable fabric marker

Glue pen

Basic sewing kit

cutting out and making the doll

Using the templates for the Basic Doll and the Vintage Waves hair, cut out, stitch, and assemble the doll, following the instructions on page 12.

belly button

1 Mark a dot for the placement of the belly button. You could do this after the swimsuit bottoms have been made and fitted—just to make sure that the bottoms don't cover the belly button.

2 Using thread that matches the skin tone and a long needle, pass the needle and thread through the center of the body from the back seam to the mark at the front. Give a small tug to pull the knot of the thread to the inside of the body.

3 Now pass the needle from front to back, inserting the needle just to the side of where it came up.

4 Repeat steps 2 and 3 once more, then pull gently: the tiny stitches will sink in to make the belly button. Take a few discrete stitches along the back seam to secure then snip the thread.

swimsuit

1 Use the template on page 122 to cut out two pattern pieces for Mia's swimsuit bottoms from striped cotton (these are not as high as the basic doll pants).

2 Follow the instructions for the doll pants on page 16.

3 Cut out Mia's swimsuit top pattern pieces from striped cotton. This is constructed in the same way as the basic bodice on page 17, but instead of turning a hem at the sleeves, snip into the seam allowance at the armholes, turn in, and sew using a backstitch. Turn in a hem at the bottom, too.

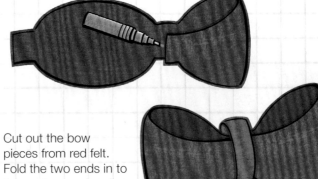

4 Cut out the bow pieces from red felt. Fold the two ends in to the center, overlapping them slightly, and secure with the glue pen. Wrap the bow band around the middle of the bow, making sure it overlaps. Secure with glue pen and, if necessary, add a few straight stitches to close. You can sew a decorative backstitch around the bow band, but this is optional. Without cutting your thread, fix the bow to the center of the swimsuit top—a few straight stitches will suffice.

flip-flops

1 Cut out all pattern pieces on page 122 from red felt. You need two sole pieces for each flip-flop, so cut out four sole pieces and two toe posts.

Tip: Good-quality felt will give you the best results here. The toe posts of the flip-flops are very fine, so you need a well-made felt that will tolerate being cut into such small shapes.

2 Using a backstitch, a fine needle, and one strand of embroidery floss (cotton), stitch around the toe post; this adds strength to this tiny piece of felt and gives a nice overall finish.

3 Place two sole pieces and one toe post piece together and then blanket stitch all the way around, stitching in the toe post as you go. The toe post may seem too big or too wide for the sole, but if you line up the sides flush with the edge of the sole as you sew around it will raise the upper part of the sandal up to fit the foot in. Start with the bottom center strap of the toe post first, then work around the rest of the sole.

4 Use a tiny bit of fabric glue to attach a little flat-back pearl to each flip-flop. Cut two small hearts from glitter fabric and glue one to each inside sole. (This looks cute, but also helps Mia to keep her flip-flops on.)

starfish

1 Cut two starfish shapes on page 122 from yellow felt. Begin by stitching some French knots and straight stitches onto one starfish piece. Use your fabric marker to draw some dots and dashes as guidelines.

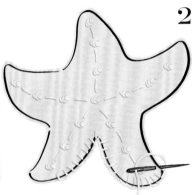

2 Place both starfish pieces wrong sides together, then blanket stitch all the way around the edge. Small stitches in a matching thread work best here. Fix to Mia's hair using some straight stitches that go through the back of the starfish and then through the hair. Repeat until the starfish is secure.

shell

1 Cut out two shell pieces on page 122 from pink felt. Using a matching thread, blanket stitch both pieces together all around the outer edge.

2 Without cutting your thread, add in the lined detail using a backstitch. Because you are sewing through two layers of felt, the stitches with sort of "sink in" a little bit to give the shell a puffy effect; this highlights the curves of the shell.

3 Use glue pen to attach a flat-back pearl to the shell and then fix to Mia's hand in the same way that you attached the starfish to her hair.

hannah

Check out Hannah's groovy flower outfit! She's wearing an A-line dress in a floral print with a peter pan collar, knee-high boots, and a huge bouffant hairstyle. Add a few Twiggy-style lashes underneath Hannah's eyes and a white Alice band to her hair to give that real '60s style.

you will need

Basic doll templates on page 110

'60s bouffant hair template on page 118

Hannah templates on page 124

Maeve boot template on page 121

Skin-tone, yellow, and black felt for the doll

Stranded embroidery floss (cotton) in assorted colors

Cotton fabric for the pants

Small length of fine elastic

'60s-style floral print cotton for the dress

White felt for the hairband, collar, and boots

Small pieces of felt for the name tag

Two snap fasteners

Washable fabric marker

Glue pen

Basic sewing kit

cutting out and making the doll

Using the templates for the Basic Doll and the '60s Bouffant hair, cut out, stitch, and assemble the doll, following the instructions on page 12. Note that you will need to add the lower lashes after embroidering the face but before you sew the head together.

lashes and hairband

1 Use the fabric marker to sketch a curved line under the eye from the outer eye inward about halfway, then draw three spiky lashes.

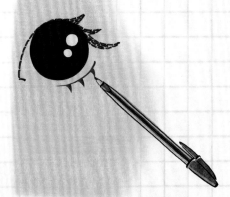

2 Sew with black thread, in much the same way as the upper lashes. Sew along the drawn lines and a base "layer" of stitching, then go back and forth with some freeform straight stitches to thicken and fill in the lines and shapes.

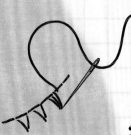

3 Using the template on page 124, cut the hairband from white felt. Fix in place with the glue pen and then backstitch around to secure.

doll pants

Follow the instructions for the doll pants on page 16.

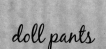

dress

1 Using the templates on page 124, cut out the dress pattern pieces from '60s-style print cotton and the collar from white felt.

2 Snip into the curved seam allowances at the neckline of the front and back pieces. Turn under and secure with glue pen. Then turn in the straight hems at the center back, and secure with the glue pen. Stitch all these hems using a backstitch.

3 Place the dress front and one of the dress back pieces right sides together and sew along the shoulder. Repeat this with the other back piece.

4 Snip into the seam allowance at the armholes. Turn a hem to the wrong side and sew around the armholes using a backstitch. Place the front and back of the dress right sides together and, without cutting the thread, sew down the side seam from the underarm to the bottom of the dress. Repeat for the other armhole and side seam.

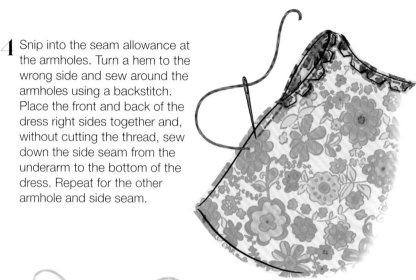

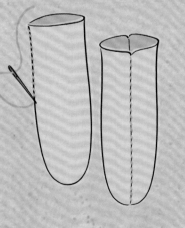

5 Turn the dress out the right way, turn in a hem along the bottom of the dress, and sew using a backstitch.

6 Add the collar to the front of the dress simply using a small whipstitch in a matching thread. Add two snap fasteners to the top half of the back of the dress.

boots

1 Using the template on page 121, cut out four boot pieces from white felt.

2 Place two boot pieces together and whipstitch all around, leaving the top open. Note that the seam on the boots is actually the front of the boot.

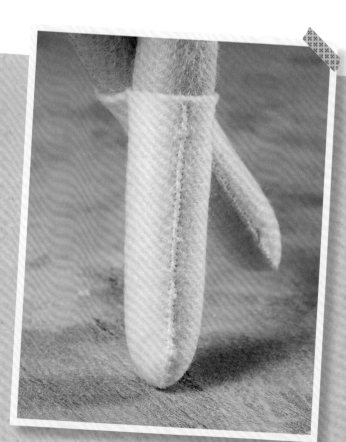

maeve

Maeve is all set to greet the trick or treaters this Halloween! Lots of layers of pretty black lace and hints of sparkly purple glitter make her witch costume the cutest ever. Maeve would also look lovely with mint green hair and emerald green glitter accents or even peach hair with bright pumpkin orange glitter. Maybe make all three and display them this October. How sweet!

you will need

Basic doll templates on page 110

Side-swept hair template on page 118

Maeve templates on page 121

Mia bow template on page 122

Skin-tone, lavender, and black felt for the doll

Stranded embroidery floss (cotton) in assorted colors

Cotton fabric for the pants

Small length of fine elastic

Lace fabric for the dress

Black, purple, brown, and tan felt for the accessories

Small pieces of felt for the name tag

Glitter fabric for bows and hat trim

Two snap fasteners

Glue pen

Basic sewing kit

cutting out and making the doll

Using the templates for the Basic Doll and the Side-swept hair, cut out, stitch, and assemble the doll, following the instructions on page 12.

doll pants

Follow the instructions for the doll pants on page 16.

dress

1 Using the templates on page 121, cut out one front bodice and two back bodice pieces from black felt. There is no need to turn in any hems or add seam allowances, as this is a strapless bodice.

2 Lay each bodice piece on top of the lace and cut around, adding ½ in. (1 cm) all around that can be turned under the bodice.

3 With right side facing up, turn the lace under each felt bodice piece and sew in place using a backstitch and matching black thread. Do this to the top of the front bodice piece and to the top and center back edges of the back pieces only. You will have excess lace on the sides and bottom of each piece; this can be trimmed later.

4 Lay the front bodice piece and one back bodice piece right sides together and sew down the side seam. Repeat for the other side and then trim the excess lace from the sides only.

5 To make the layered lace skirt, begin by cutting three strips of lace, each 20 in. (50 cm) long but with three different widths: 3 in. (8 cm), 4 in. (10 cm), and 5 in. (12.5 cm). Lay them on top of each other, lining them up at the top. Baste (tack) along the top in a contrasting color to hold the layers together; the basting (tacking) stitches can be removed once the bodice and skirt have been sewn together.

6 Add the skirt to the bodice in the same way as most of the other doll dresses. Place the bodice and the skirt strip right sides together and sew, adding pleats as you go, make two or three stitches between each pleat. You may not use all 20 in. (50 cm) of the layered lace.

7 Trim any excess from the length of the skirt and from the waistband. Remove the basting (tacking) stitches. Finish the edges at either end of the skirt and add two snap fasteners to the bodice.

Tip: Using some wide lace trim really helps here; I used some inexpensive trim that was scalloped at either edge. I used these scallops in the layered skirt of the dress. No raw edges to finish!

bat cape

1 Using the templates on page 121, cut one cape back and two fronts from purple felt. Place the back and one front right sides together and backstitch down the shoulder and side. Repeat for the other side.

2 Turn out the right way and, using a contrasting thread, sew around the edges using a running stitch.

boots

1 Using the template on page 121, cut out four boot pieces from black felt.

2 Place two pieces together and whipstitch all around, leaving the top open (there is no need to turn out the right way). Repeat for the other boot.

3 Using the template on page 121, cut out two small bows and two small rectangles for the centers from glitter fabric. Fold each side of each bow in to the center and secure with glue pen. Wrap the center rectangle around the middle and secure with glue pen, too.

4 Add a few stitches to the back of the bow and, without cutting the thread, attach to the front of the boot, with the seam of the boot at the front.

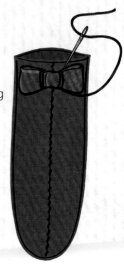

Tip: Often the reverse of glitter fabric is white, so to disguise this and give a nice finish, try coloring the edges and any parts of the white reverse fabric that will be seen with a matching colored marker or gel pen.

broomstick

1 Cut a piece of brown felt about 7 x 1 in. (18 x 2.5 cm). Generously apply glue pen to one side of the felt and then roll the felt up as tightly as you can so that you end up with a long roll. You may have to hold or pinch it for a minute or two until the glue takes.

2 Give the roll of felt a firm tug a few times, and it should stretch a bit (don't worry if it doesn't); this gives quite a bit of strength to the felt and makes it stiffer. Pinch one end flat and cut on the diagonal; this will be the top end of the broom. Whipstitch down the length to secure the felt roll; pulling the stitches fairly taut will give added strength, too.

3 Using the template on page 121, cut out two broom head pieces from tan or pale yellow felt. Line them up together and whipstitch around, starting from the top.

4 Before finishing the whipstitch and without cutting your thread, add a pinch of stuffing into the broom, just enough to make it puffy (overstuffing will distort the shape). Insert the broom handle and continue whipstitching to close and secure. Take a few straight stitches through the broom and the broom handle.

hat

1 Using the templates on page 121, cut out the "cone" and brim from black felt. Cut the hat trim and bow from the glitter fabric, using the Mia bow template on page 122.

2 Whipstitch the two straight edges of the cone together using a matching black thread. Pinch and "twirl" the pointy end so that it will bend slightly.

3 Add a small amount of stuffing to the inside of the hat. (This is only to add some structure so that the hat doesn't cave inward—overstuffing will distort the shape.) Whipstitch the cone to the brim of the hat; it's a good idea to place the cone on the brim and make some guide marks with a white fabric pencil to keep the cone centered.

4 Using a glue pen, stick the glitter trim around the base of the cone. Make the bow following the instructions for Mia's bow on page 36, and glue in place.

anna

Needless to say, Anna loves books! So much so, in fact, that she became a librarian. She always has her nose buried in an old volume—the Brontë sisters are her favorites. Anna wears a smart pencil skirt, coupled with a floaty-sleeved blouse that has pretty pearl buttons. Her fabulous '50s-style glasses frame her lovely face and complement her elegant top knot.

you will need

Basic doll templates on page 110

Top-knit hair template on page 119

Anna templates on page 112

Mia, Robyn, and Hannah templates on pages 122 and 124

Skin tone, yellow, and black felt for the doll

Stranded embroidery floss (cotton) in assorted colors

Cotton or lace fabric for the pants

Small length of fine elastic

Polka dot cotton for blouse

Plain cotton for the skirt

Felt for the shoes, bow, and collar

Three pearl beads

Three snap fasteners

Glue pen

Basic sewing kit

cutting out and making the doll

Using the templates for the Basic Doll and the Top-knot hair, cut out, stitch, and assemble the doll, following the instructions on page 12. Note that Anna's hair goes over one eye, so you will need to sketch and stitch the eyes before attaching the hair.

doll pants

Follow the instructions for the doll pants on page 16. If you like, you can make the doll pants from lace instead of cotton.

shoes

Use the templates for the Pointy Shoe on page 111 to cut out two soles and two uppers from black felt. Follow the instructions on page 16 to complete the shoes.

bow

Use the templates for Mia's bow on page 122 to cut the pieces from felt, and then follow the instructions on page 38 to make a bow. Without cutting your thread, fix the bow in position by stitching through the doll's hair.

blouse

1 Using the Robyn's blouse templates on page 121, cut out two back bodices, one front bodice, and two sleeves from polka dot cotton fabric. Make the blouse, following the instructions for Robyn's blouse on page 64.

2 Using the Hannah's collar template on page 121, cut out the collar from white felt and attach it to the neckline using whipstitch and a matching white thread. Stitch the pearl buttons to the front of the blouse.

skirt

1 Using the templates on page 112, cut out one skirt front and two skirt backs from plain cotton. Anna's skirt has four pleats—two at the front and one on either side at the back. Mark the position of the pleats on your pattern pieces.

2 Place the front and one back piece right sides together and sew down the side seam. Snip a few notches into the curve. Repeat with the other back piece.

3 Fold in a ¼-in. (5-mm) hem at each center back edge of the skirt—don't sew or use any glue pen.

4 Now you need to fold the pleats in toward the center. Measure your doll's waist (usually around 6 in./15 cm) and keep trying the skirt on the doll as you adjust the pleats to ensure a nice fit. Use pins to hold the pleats while you do this. When you are happy with the fit, use a basting (tacking) stitch in a contrast thread to hold the pleats in place.

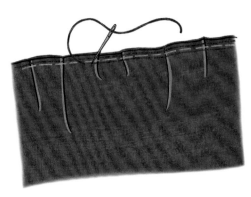

5 Now fold down the waistband by ¼ in. (5 mm). Run two lines of backstitch across to give a faux waistband effect and then remove the basting stitches.

6 With right sides together, line up the two edges (with the hems folded in) and pin. Sew along the center part of this back seam for about 2½ in. (6 cm), leaving an opening for the leg split and a similar opening at the top to help give a good fit at the waist.

7 Turn the skirt out the right way and finish the seams at the split and the opening at the waistband.

8 Turn under and stitch a ¼-in. (5-mm) hem at the bottom of the skirt, then try the skirt on your doll and mark where you want the snap fastener to be. Add the snap fastener.

glasses

1 Anna's glasses are molded from a piece of felt "tape." Begin by cutting a piece of felt ½ in. (1 cm) wide and around 10 in. (25 cm) long.

2 Add a generous helping of the glue pen to the surface of one side and fold the felt in half lengthwise. Place a book on top, pinch, or use pins until the glue takes—you don't want it to completely dry, but you want it to hold the felt in half.

3 Now gently pull along the length of the felt; you will notice that it thins out slightly and becomes much stronger.

Tip: This technique of making felt "tape" or "ribbon" is really handy to know. It is great for bag handles, hair accessories, belts etc.

4 Mold the felt into a basic spectacles shape; keep trying it on the doll to make sure the fit is right.

5 Once the fit is right and the shape is fairly symmetrical, add a few stitches in the center just to hold everything in place. Trim off any excess and use a small piece of this excess to wrap around the center, stitching at the back and then through the center to really secure the center of the glasses.

6 Add the points by pinching a fold and securing with a few stitches in a matching thread.

7 Attach the glasses to the face by first securing the center, using stitches that loop around the frame of the glasses. Do the same to the top and bottom of each half of the glasses. If you use matching thread and stay very close to the glasses frame, it will be hard to detect these stitches.

lyra

Spring is in the air and Lyra is off to the farmer's market to fill her shopping basket with lots of lovely fruit and vegetables. Her dress is in a boat-neck style but uses a different bodice to give a lower waistband—just a subtle difference, but it gives a whole new look!

you will need

Basic doll templates on page 110

Wavy hair template on page 119

Edie crop top templates on page 114

Isla basket templates on page 120

Skin-tone, brown, and black felt for the doll

Stranded embroidery floss (cotton) in assorted colors

Striped cotton fabric for the pants

Small length of fine elastic

Floral cotton fabric for the dress

Felt for the shoes and basket

Small piece of cotton for inside the basket

Two snap fasteners

Glue pen

Basic sewing kit

cutting out and making the doll

Using the templates for the Basic Doll and the Wavy hair, cut out, stitch, and assemble the doll, following the instructions on page 12.

doll pants

Follow the instructions for the doll pants on page 16 to make shorts from denim fabric.

shoes

Use the Pointy Shoe templates on page 111 to cut out two soles and two uppers from pink felt. Follow the instructions on page 16 to complete the shoes.

basket

Follow the instructions for Isla's basket on page 103 to make a basket for Lyra from pale blue felt.

dress

For Lyra's dress follow Steps 1–4 of Lily's dress on page 33, but use Edie's crop top templates on page 114 for the bodice. All other instructions are the same.

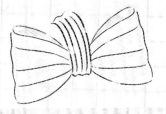

cool & cute

penny

Penny's skinny jeans are so skinny that they are actually part of her body! You'll need to make the doll in a slightly different way, using the denim fabric for part of her body and legs, before continuing with the rest of the body in the usual way.

body and skinny jeans

1 Using the Penny templates on page 123, cut out one upper body front, two upper body backs, and four feet from skin-tone felt. Cut one skinny jean front, two skinny jean backs, and four skinny jean legs from denim fabric. Place the upper body front and skinny jean front right sides together and stitch using a ¼-in. (5-mm) seam allowance to create one complete front body pattern piece.

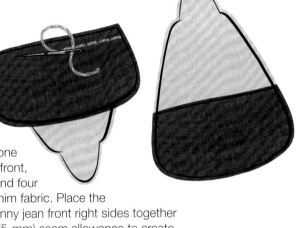

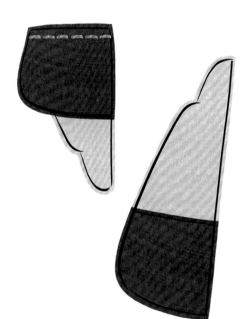

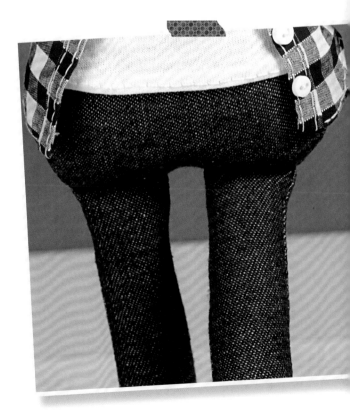

2 Continue in the same way for the two halves of the back body pieces, sewing the upper body back to the skinny jeans back, again using a ¼-in. (5-mm) seam allowance.

3 Attach a foot piece to a skinny jeans leg in the same way and repeat to make four leg pieces.

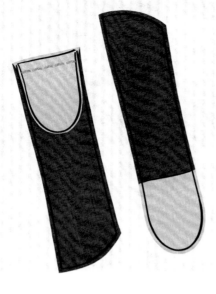

4 Cut out the remaining body pattern pieces, using the arm, neck, head, and eye Basic Doll templates on page 110 and the Ponytail hair template on page 119. Now that you have all the body pattern pieces, follow the instructions for the Basic Doll on page 12 to make the body, limbs, face, and hair and then stuff and assemble, ready for dressing.

white tee

Using the t-shirt templates on page 123, make Penny's white tee, following the basic bodice instructions on page 17. Stitch a hem along the bottom of the t-shirt.

w shirt

1 Using the templates on page 123, cut out two shirt fronts, one shirt back, two shirt sleeves, and two collars from gingham or plaid fabric.

2 Take the two shirt fronts and fold and backstitch a small hem around the necklines to the wrong side on each one. For the button panels, turn a double ¼ in. (5 mm) hem— but this time to the right side of the fabric. Sew a line of stitching up each side of the button panel, using backstitch and matching sewing thread.

3 Attach the shirt fronts to the shirt back by sewing them together across the shoulder

4 Add the sleeves by placing one sleeve and the shirt body right sides together, lining up the edges around the armhole. Backstitch with approx. ⅛ in. (3 mm) seam allowance, folding three small pleats at the top of the armhole. Repeat for the other sleeve.

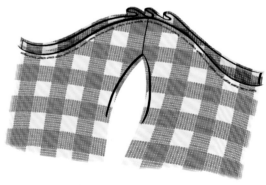

5 Now place the front and back of your shirt right sides together again, and line up the sleeves and sides. Sew along the sleeve from the "cuff" to the underarm and from the underarm down the side of the shirt. Repeat for the other side and turn out the right way.

6 Snip into the seam allowance of the two curved sides of the collar pieces, then fold to the wrong side and secure with the glue pen and stitch around. Do not fold in the seam allowance along the top of the collar, as you will use this to stitch the collar to the neckline.

7 Place one collar at the neckline, pointing upward, so that the right side of the shirt and the wrong side of the collar are facing you. Sew along, following the seam allowance of the collar to attach to the neckline, then fold the collar down the right way. Repeat with the other collar piece.

8 Snip into the curves at the hemline of the shirt, turn in and secure with the glue pen. Backstitch around the bottom of the shirt.

9 Turn up the sleeves using a small double hem and sew a double line of stitching to match the stitching on the button panel.

10 Add five ⅛ in. (4 mm) buttons down one side of the button panel.

sneakers

1 Using the templates on page 123, cut two sneaker uppers and two sneaker soles from red felt and two sneaker toes from white felt. Attach the white toes to the upper sneakers using a small backstitch.

2 With two or three strands of white embroidery floss (cotton), take three large stitches with a French knot at each end to create the "laces."

3 Place the sneaker upper and sneaker sole right sides together and sew all around, leaving the top of the sneaker open. Push out the seam to get a nice clean curve to the sneaker.

kate

It's freezing outside but Kate doesn't mind; she can't wait to put on her brand-new red winter coat and snuggly boots! Her woolly hat, scarf, and mittens are sure to keep her warm and cozy as she plays in the snow with her pals. If knitting is not your thing, then you could try crocheting Kate's accessories, or you could use a lovely felt, an old sweater, or even some of the furry fabric left over from Kate's boots! Just crochet or cut out to the dimensions given; if you are using fabric (such as felt or an old garment), just snip into the ends of the scarf for tassels.

body and skinny jeans

Kate is wearing skinny jeans so she is put together in the same way as Penny. Follow steps 1–4 on pages 57–58, using the Side-swept hair on page 118.

floral top

Make Kate's floral top using Penny's t-shirt templates on page 123 and following the basic bodice instructions on page 17. Stitch a hem along the bottom of the t-shirt.

coat

1 Kate's coat is put together using the same steps as Olivia's duffle coat, but with a few small adjustments, such as a collar instead of a hood. Using the Olivia duffle coat templates on page 121, cut one coat back, two coat fronts, and two sleeves from red felt. Follow steps 2–6 on page 98 to make the main body of the coat, turning under a small hem around the bottom of the coat and backstitching this as well.

2 Using the Lily templates on page 120, cut out all the collar pieces from red felt. Take two collar front pieces and place them together, using the glue pen to fix them in place while you sew. Stitch around the bottom edges using a backstitch. Repeat this process for the opposite front collar and the back collar, too.

3 Using a matching thread to the coat color, whipstitch the collar pieces in place around the neckline of the coat. Keep your stitches small, but make sure that you sew through all layers of the neckline and collar.

4 Cut two pocket pieces from red felt. Use two pins placed in opposite directions to secure the pcokets to the front of the coat (you can remove the pins once you have started stitching). Backstitch around the bottom of the pockets.

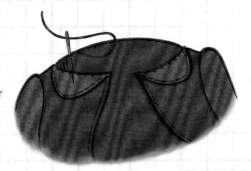

5 Try the coat on your doll to check the fit, particularly around the neckline. If it seems too wide, you can add a few stitches on either side using matching thread.

6 Turn up the sleeves by ¼–½ in. (5–8 mm), again checking on your doll for fit. Backstitch around the edges.

7 Add the three buttons down the left coat front. Using some small embroidery scissors, make small snips into the right coat front for buttonholes—start off small, don't be tempted to make large cuts.

Tip: The top of the pocket is trimmed with scalloped fabric scissors. If you don't have these, you can always draw on a few scallop shapes with a washable fabric marker and cut them out using small embroidery scissors.

boots

1 Using the Noah templates on page 122, cut four boot pieces from faux suede (alternatively you could use felt) and cut four pieces of faux lambswool fabric approximately 2 x 1 in. (5 x 2.5 cm). This is deliberately too big and will be trimmed later.

2 Take one lambswool piece and place it right side down. Take one boot piece and place it right side up, overlapping slightly by around ⅛ in. (3 mm). Stitch the two fabrics together by sewing across the boot top (these stitches won't be seen); a backstitch will be perfect here. Repeat for the other three boot pieces.

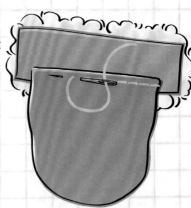

3 Take two of these pieces and place them right sides together. When placed correctly you will see the wrong side of the faux suede and the right side of the faux lambswool. Sew all around the side and bottom of the boot, leaving a few millimeters of the lambswool unstitched.

4 Trim away any excess lambswool, but still leave it a few millimeters wider that the faux suede. Turn out the right way. Push out the curved seam to get a nice clean shape. Now turn down the lambswool and, if need be, add a stitch or two to join the edges of the lambswool on either side (you may find that the fabric is fluffy enough and this step is not needed). Repeat steps 3–4 to make the other boot.

scarf

Finished measurement: 1 x 12 in.
(2.5 x 30 cm)

1 Cast on 8 stitches.

2 Knit every row for approximately
12 in. (30 cm).

3 Bind (cast) off and weave in ends.

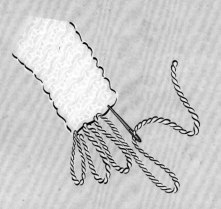

4 Using a darning needle and a
length of yarn, thread some long
loops at either end of the scarf.

5 Now trim these loops to around
1 in. (2.5 cm).

hat

Finished measurement: 5 in. (12.5 cm) wide by 2 in. (5 cm) high

1 Cast on 34 stitches.

2 Rib stitch for 4 rows (i.e. knit 1, purl
1 to the end of each row).

3 Stockinette (stocking) stitch (i.e. knit
1 row, purl 1 row) for 5 in. (12cm).

4 Rib stitch again for 4 rows.

5 Bind (cast) off and weave in ends.

6 Fold in half with right sides together
and stitch each side, curving the
corners as you go. Use the darning
needle and the same knitting yarn
instead of thread. Your stitches do
not need to be neat. Turn out the
right way.

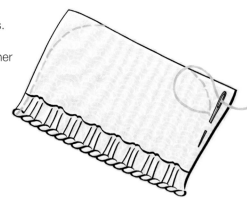

mittens

Finished measurement: 1 x 1 in. (2.5 x 2.5 cm). Kate's
mittens are put together in the same way as the hat, just
using different measurements.

1 Cast on 8 stitches.

2 Rib stitch for 4 rows.

3 Stockinette (stocking) stitch for 2 in. (5 cm).

4 Rib stitch for 4 rows.

5 Bind (cast) off and weave in ends.

6 Fold in half with right sides together and stitch each
side, curving the corners as you go.

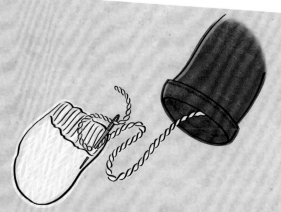

7 Attach a long piece of yarn to one mitten.
Using the darning needle and matching yarn, take
a few stitches on one side of the cuff. Then thread
that yarn through one arm, across the back of the
coat, and through the other arm. Try on your doll to
get the length right, then attach the other mitten in
the same way.

robyn

Robyn is just cute as a button in her denim dungarees, ditzy floral floaty-sleeved blouse, and adorable double-bun hairdo! You could also team these dungarees with Penny's white t-shirt or with a little crop top like the one Ruby or Edie wears.

you will need

Basic doll templates on page 110

Double-bun hair template on page 118

Robyn templates on page 124

Noah jeans template on page 122

Skin-tone and black felt for the doll

Stranded embroidery floss (cotton) in assorted colors

Lightweight cotton denim

Cotton for the shirt

Felt for the shoes

Small pieces of felt for the name tag

Two ⅛-in. (4-mm) buttons

Two snap fasteners

Four pearl beads

Small length of fine elastic

Glue pen

Basic sewing kit

cutting out and making the doll

Using the templates for the Basic Doll and the Double Bun hair, cut out, stitch, and assemble the doll, following the instructions on page 12.

shoes

1 Use the Pointy Shoe templates on page 111 to cut out two soles and two uppers from felt. Follow the instructions on page 16 to complete the shoes.

blouse

1 Using the templates for Robyn's blouse on page 121 cut out two backs, one front, and two sleeves from cotton fabric.

2 Robyn's blouse is put together in the same way as the bodice and sleeve combo explained in Kayla's dress on page 107—this blouse is just a longer version of Kayla's bodice. Hem along the bottom to finish.

dungarees

1 Using the Noah jeans template on page 122, cut two pieces from denim fabric. Once you have cut out the two jeans pieces, cut a ¾-in. (2-cm) strip off the waistband of each piece before you start sewing the jeans together. These strips will be used for the straps later. This also means that the jeans aren't so high-waisted and are therefore a better shape for dungarees! Follow the instructions on page 96 to stitch the dungarees.

2 Add elastic to the waist as you would to make doll pants (see page 16). Turn the jeans the right way out.

3 Using the template on page 124, cut out the dungaree bib from denim fabric. Turn under the hems on both sides and along the top and then backstitch to secure.

4 Place the bib upside down on top of the jeans, so that the wrong side of the bib is facing you and the top of the bib is pointing down. Sew across the bottom of the bib using a backstitch.

5 Take the two ¾-in. (2-cm) strips, fold each long side in to the center of the wrong side, and secure with glue pen. You could sew along each strap, but this is optional.

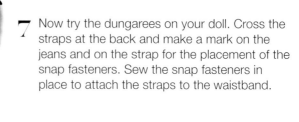

6 Sew one end of each strap to the top corners of the dungaree bib: place the strap underneath and the button on top and then stitch through the button, bib, and strap until they feel secure.

7 Now try the dungarees on your doll. Cross the straps at the back and make a mark on the jeans and on the strap for the placement of the snap fasteners. Sew the snap fasteners in place to attach the straps to the waistband.

pearl hair ties

Simply thread two pearl beads onto some fine elastic. Tie in a double or triple knot and trim the excess. You now have a mini hair bobble. Wind one around each of Robyn's hair buns.

Sweet Maisie is wearing a cool boat neck dress made from denim and a cute little diamond print. Pink neon glitter shoes and a matching bow in her turquoise hair sets her outfit off perfectly. Maisie's dress is really versatile so play around with textures and prints for lots of different effects.

you will need

Basic doll templates on page 110

Long bob hair template on page 118

Maisie template on page 120

Skin-tone cotton fabric for the body and head

Turquoise felt for the hair

Stranded embroidery floss (cotton) in assorted colors

Cotton fabric for the doll pants

Small length of fine elastic

Lightweight denim fabric for the dress

Contrast print cotton for the "skirt"

Glitter fabric for the shoes and hair bow

Two snap fasteners

One flat-back pearl or button

Small pieces of felt and small piece of cotton for name tag and pocket

Glue pen

Basic sewing kit

cutting out and making the doll

To make this larger size doll, you will need to enlarge the templates for the Basic Doll by 180% and the Long Bob hair by 380% to create a doll that is approximately 24 in. (60 cm) tall. Use these templates to cut the body, head, neck, arms, and legs from skin-tone cotton. Cut the hair from turquoise felt. Follow the instructions for Heidi's face and body on page 105 to make the doll, remembering to use a ¼-in. (5-mm) seam allowance.

doll pants

Enlarge the doll pants templates by 180% as before and cut the pattern pieces from your cotton fabric. Follow the instructions on page 16 to complete the pants.

shoes

Enlarge the Basic Shoe template on page 111 by 180% and cut two soles and two uppers from glitter fabric. It is probably worth checking the size against your finished doll's foot to make sure it will be a snug fit. Follow the instructions on page 16 to complete the shoes.

dress

1 Follow steps 1–4 of Lily's dress on page 33, enlarging the bodice templates by 180% before you cut the pattern pieces. Cut a strip of print cotton that is 6 x 20 in. (15 x 50 cm) for the skirt part of the dress. You may not need all 20 in. (50 cm) of the fabric, depending on how many pleats you add.

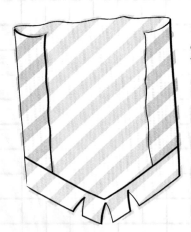

2 Using the template on page 120, cut out the pocket in a contrasting color or print. Turn in the hems at the sides, securing with the glue pen. Snip around the point before turning under also.

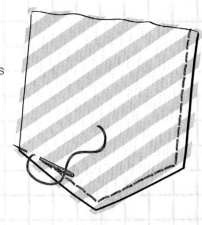

3 Stitch around the pocket edges using a backstitch; there is no need to sew along the top.

4 Position the pocket on the bodice of the dress so that the pocket points upward and stitch in place.

5 Fold the pocket down into the correct position and either add a flat-back pearl with some fabric glue or sew on a small button.

bow

Follow the instructions on page 38 to make a bow from glitter fabric and attach it to Maisie's hair.

you will need

Girl Squad templates on pages 116–117

Skin-tone, brown, yellow, and black felt for the dolls and hairstyles

Stranded embroidery floss (cotton) in assorted colors

Cotton fabric for dresses and pants

⅛-in. (4-mm) buttons

Fine elastic

Felt for shoes and flowers

Glue pen

Basic sewing kit

This is my girl squad: Farrah, Brianna, Saoirse, and Maggie! You can make your own squad, too, as these little dolls are fully customizable; choose your own hairstyle, color scheme, and lipstick color. Make your best friends, your sisters, cousins, aunties, classmates, workmates, or even your bridesmaids. The possibilities are endless. Make an entire posse of your nearest and dearest.

cutting out and making the dolls

The best thing about these mini dolls —they are only 9 in. (22 cm) tall—is that they are quick to make and you only need little pieces of cotton and felt. So you could use up all your scraps and leftovers from making the other dolls in the book! They are put together in the same way as their larger versions, so use the templates given on pages 166–117 but follow the instructions for the Basic Doll, Doll Pants, Basic Bodice, and Basic Shoe on pages 12–16. The rose is made in the same way as that in Edie's hair on page 89, step 2.

The only difference between the mini dolls and the larger ones is the eyes; here they are small ovals. For this, just follow the same method used before for the eyes and lashes.

TIP: Attach the little ovals with glue pen as soon as you have cut them out and use a small whipstitch all the way around; because this is such a tiny piece of felt, the fibers might shed and you could lose definition, so don't let it hang around too long before you sew around the edges

TIPS
for sewing tiny things:
Use a fine needle and thread or one strand of embroidery floss (cotton) and remember that small, regular stitches are so important here; the more your needle and thread goes through the felt, the stronger your seams will be. This is especially helpful when turning mini limbs and bodies out the right way.

Stuff until quite firm; this will give nice smooth shapes to the doll body.

Customize the dresses by adding buttons, bows, lace, or ribbon. Make them fuller, longer, or shorter by adjusting the amount of fabric you use for the skirt of the dress.

attaching fastenings

Even the smallest snap fastener can be too bulky for these little dresses. You could use a piece of Velcro to close the bodice at the back or you could tie a piece of fine elastic into a loop and close with a ⅛ in. (4-mm) button. Here's how:

1 Use the end of a pencil to tie a small loop of elastic, pull it taut, and double or treble knot it.

2 Remove from the pencil and trim the tails, leaving at least ¼ in. (5 mm).

3 Attach to one side of the bodice on the wrong side (where you would normally place a snap fastener). Stitch in place, making sure that the thread and needle go around each side of the knot. Add another loop at the bottom of the bodice.

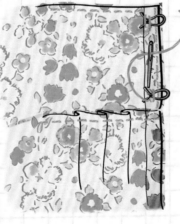

4 Add buttons to the opposite side of the bodice back to correspond with the elastic loops.

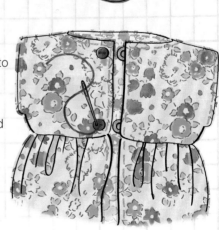

ella

Ella's denim shorts and floral blouse create the perfect combo for a day in the park with her friends! She is also a great example of how you can mix and match all the different patterns and designs in the book to make new outfits!

you will need

Basic doll templates on page 110

Long bob hair template on page 118

Elise blouse templates on page 113

Mia bow templates on page 122

Skin-tone and black felt for the doll

Stranded embroidery floss (cotton) in assorted colors

Cotton denim fabric for the shorts

Small length of fine elastic

Cotton fabric for the blouse

Small pieces of felt for the shoes, name tag, and bow

Two snap fasteners

Three ⅛-in. (4-mm) buttons

Glue pen

Basic sewing kit

Tip: If you ever find yourself stuck for what color to use for your doll's accessories—whether shoes, buttons, bows, flowers, or bags—pick a few colors of felt that match your main fabric and "audition" them next to each other. The right one for your color scheme will jump right out at you! If you feel you have too many colors already, then navy or black is always a great option for shoes and bags.

cutting out and making the doll

Using the templates for the Basic Doll and the Long Bob hair, cut out, stitch, and assemble the doll, following the instructions on page 12.

doll pants

Follow the instructions for the doll pants on page 16 to make shorts from denim fabric.

bow

Use the templates for Mia's bow on page 122 to cut the pieces from felt and then follow the instructions on page 38 to make a bow. Without cutting your thread, fix the bow in position by stitching through the doll's hair.

shoes

Using the Pointy Shoe templates on page 111, cut out two soles and two uppers from black felt. Follow the instructions on page 16 to complete the shoes.

v-neck blouse

Refer to the instructions for Elise's V-neck blouse on page 28 to make a floral blouse for Ella. Note that Ella's blouse has three decorative buttons down the front.

sophie

Sophie is off to the prom this evening and she's wearing her dream dress—a base of pretty coral/peach cotton, layers of sheer blush tulle and an over layer of soft white polka dot tulle, off set with an oversized bow and some sparkly shoes. Of course, she added a beautiful bloom to her elegant chignon. Have a great time at the prom, Sophie!

you will need

Basic doll templates on page 110

Side-bun hair template on page 119

Edie rose and petal templates on page 115

Maeve strapless bodice templates on page 121

Skin-tone, brown, and black felt for the doll

Stranded embroidery floss (cotton) in assorted colors

Cotton fabric for the pants

Small length of fine elastic

Peach/coral cotton for the under layer of the dress

Blush tulle for the mid-layers

White polka dot tulle for the over layer

Felt for the rose and name tag

Gold glitter fabric for the shoes and leaf

Two snap fasteners

Glue pen

Basic sewing kit

cutting out and making the doll

Using the templates for the Basic Doll and the Side-bun hair, cut out, stitch, and assemble the doll, following the instructions on page 12.

doll pants

Follow the instructions for the doll pants on page 16

shoes

Use the Pointy Shoe templates on page 111 to cut out two soles and two uppers from gold glitter fabric. Follow the instructions on page 16 to complete the shoes.

dress

Tip: When buying tulle for your doll projects, always look for the soft or "veiling" option. Some tutu fabric can be quite stiff and will add too much bulk to a small doll garment. Soft tulle (used for wedding veils) drapes well, doesn't stick to or pull felt, and is much more pleasant to handle!

1 Using the Maeve templates on page 121, cut out the strapless bodice pieces from peach cotton, adding a ¼-in. (5-mm) seam allowance to the top and sides. Fold in these seam allowances but don't sew.

2 Cover each bodice piece with the polka dot tulle by laying each bodice piece on top of the tulle and cutting out, adding about ½ in. (1 cm) all around.

3 Fold the tulle into the top edge of the front bodice piece, and sew across using a backstitch. You can use either a contrasting or matching thread. Repeat for the top and center back hems of the back bodice pieces. Note: any overhanging lace will be trimmed off later.

4 Place the front bodice and one of the back bodice pieces right sides together. Sew down the side seam. Repeat for the other side. You can now trim the excess tulle from the side only (the excess tulle is to ensure that it doesn't slip out of place while the dress is put together).

5 The "skirt" of Sophie's prom dress has four layers: one layer of peach cotton, two layers of blush coloured tulle, and an over layer of polka dot tulle. Begin by cutting a strip of the cotton measuring 20 x 6 in. (50 x 15 cm). Cut the strips of tulle and polka dot tulle just a little bigger and lay them on top of the cotton, lining them up at the top. Use a basting (tacking) or running stitch along the top in a contrasting color to hold the layers together while you attach the bodice.

6 Now place the bodice and the skirt right sides together, leaving ¼ in. (5 mm) at the beginning to turn in a hem later. Sew across, adding pleats as you go. The pleats here will be deeper, as the layers of fabric are thicker than a single layer of cotton.

7 Trim the excess tulle from the waist and any excess from the skirt, making sure to leave around ¼ in. (5 mm) at the side and bottom edges to turn under for a hem.

Tip: If you have them, use pinking shears or scalloped scissors to cut the tulle. This will give a nice finished edge that doesn't need to be hemmed.

Tip: Add more layers to give a fuller look. You could also adjust the length of the dress or even play around with the hem. Sew a larger hem on the cotton layer and let the tulle hang longer or even trim the tulle shorter than the cotton. You could even change the position of the bow.

rose

Refer to Edie on page 89, step 2, to make a rose. Make it larger for Sophie by adding some extra petals.

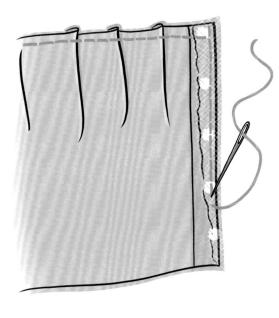

8 Turn in hems at each end of the skirt. Ease out the tulle near the bottom of the dress, so that the cotton hem is still ¼ in. (5 mm) but the tulle layers gradually end up as a hem of only a few millimeters. This ensures that the bottom of the dress stays flouncy and isn't restricted.

9 For the bow, cut two strips of polka dot tulle around 6 x 3 in. (15 x 8 cm). Layer them on top of each other and sew together across the two short ends. Turn the right way out so that the seams are on the inside of the loop.

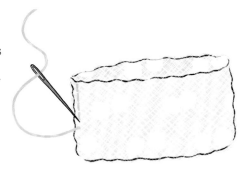

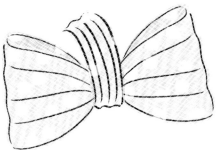

10 Adjust the loop so that the seams are in the center. Cut a smaller strip of dot tulle, gather it together to make a thinner strip, and wrap it around the middle of the larger piece. It might help to gather the larger piece in the middle also. Pull tightly and add a few stitches to the back to secure. Trim off any excess and attach to the front of the bodice. Fan out the loops of the bow to give a full, oversized look.

11 Add two snap fasteners to the back of the bodice. Hem the cotton layer only at the bottom of the dress. Remember to fluff out the tulle as a finishing touch.

zara

Zara loves to throw on her trusty artist's smock and lock herself away in her art studio, painting for hours on end. Her linen overall is an unusual shape, with a lovely curved hem and three-quarter length sleeves.

cutting out and making the doll

Zara is wearing skinny jeans, so refer to Penny on page 57 to put her body together. The hairstyle used here is Side Swept.

shoes

Use the templates for the Basic Shoe on page 111 to cut out two soles and two uppers from black felt. Follow the instructions on page 16 to complete the shoes.

you will need

Basic doll templates on page 110

Penny templates on page 123

Side-swept hair template on page 118

Zara templates on page 125

Skin-tone, brown, and black felt for the body

Lightweight denim fabric for the skinny jeans

Stranded embroidery floss (cotton) in assorted colors

Natural-colored linen or cotton for the smock

Black felt for the shoes

Small pieces of felt for name tag, paintbrush, and palette

Two snap fasteners

Acrylic paint (optional)

Glue pen

Basic sewing kit

smock

1 Using the templates on page 125, cut out all the smock pieces from linen fabric. Snip into the curved seam allowances around the necklines of the front and back bodice pieces, then turn in the straight center back hems on both back bodice pieces. Secure with glue pen and backstitch.

2 Place the front and one back bodice piece right sides together and sew along the shoulder seam. Repeat for the other sleeve.

3 Turn in and sew a small hem at the end of each sleeve.

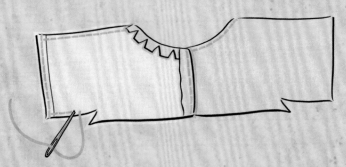

4 With the bodice still right sides together, stitch up from the cuff of the sleeve to the underarm and then from the underarm down the side seam. Trim the seam at the underarm point before turning out the right way.

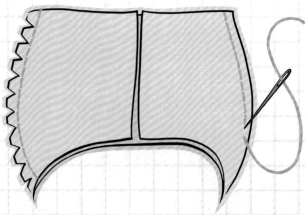

5   Now for the smock "skirt": place the front piece and one back piece right sides together. Using a ¼-in. (5-mm) seam, sew down the side and then snip into the curved seam allowance. Repeat for the other side.

6   Turn a hem at each end, secure with the glue pen, and backstitch.

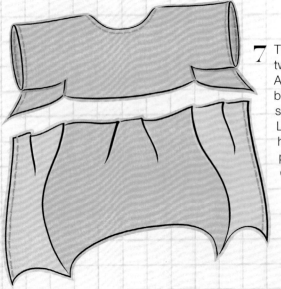

7   There are four deep pleats to be added to the smock: two on the front and one on either side at the back. Add these pleats to the skirt before attaching it to the bodice and secure in place with a basting (tacking) stitch in a contrasting thread that will be removed later. Line up the side seams on the bodice and the skirt to help determine the depth of the pleats. Fold the front pleats so that they face each other and the two back ones in the same way.

8   Snip into the curved seam allowance of the pocket and turn under, but don't sew. Fold down a small hem at the top of the pocket and sew this across with a backstitch.

9   Cut some small pieces of brown and gray felt for the paintbrush, play around with the placement of the brush, with the pocket over the top of it. Then secure the paintbrush with the glue pen. (You could stitch it into place, but with such tiny pieces of felt the glue will suffice.) Sew down the sides and around the bottom of the pocket.

10   Turn in a hem at the bottom of the smock. Snip into the seam allowances to give a nice curved hemline. Add two snap fasteners at the back of the smock.

paint palette

1 Using the template on page 125, cut two palette pieces from brown felt; two layers gives strength and holds the shape better.

2 Stitch the two pieces together by first sewing around the thumbhole, then sew around the outside of the palette using a backstitch. Add some acrylic paint or small pieces of felt. Attach to the doll's hand by passing the needle and thread through the back of the palette and then through the doll's arm for a short distance, then through the back of the palette again. Repeat this until it feels secure.

trendy & hip

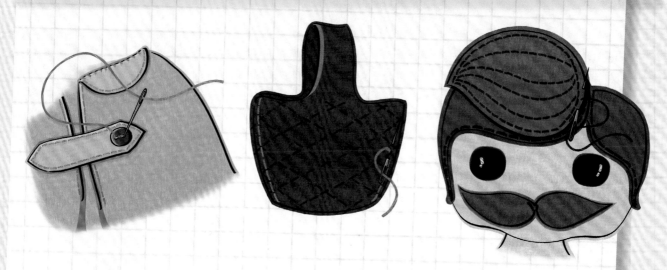

edie

Edie's favorite thing to do is to see all her best-loved bands at the biggest summer festivals. She loves music! Her outfit is ideal for keeping her cool and comfy: simple denim shorts and a crop top, layered with a pretty lace gilet, faux suede tassel boots, a slouchy bag and, of course, the quintessential flower crown!

you will need

Basic doll templates on page 110

Side-swept hair template on page 118

Edie templates on page 114

Skin-tone, red, and black felt for the doll

Stranded embroidery floss (cotton) in assorted colors

Small print floral cotton fabric for the crop top

Denim fabric for the shorts

Small length of fine elastic

Lace fabric at least 6 in. (15 cm) wide for the gilet

Suedette or faux suede for the tassel bag and boots

Snap fastener

Felt scraps in assorted colors for the flower crown

Glue pen

Basic sewing kit

cutting out and making the doll

Using the templates for the Basic Doll and the Side-swept hair, cut out, stitch, and assemble the doll, following the instructions on page 12.

crop top

Use the crop top templates on page 114 to cut the front and back pieces from the floral fabric. Follow the basic bodice instructions on page 17 to make the crop top. Hem the bottom edge of the crop top, too.

denim shorts

Follow the instructions for the doll pants on page 16

lace gilet

1 Cut the gilet pattern pieces on page 115 from the lace fabric. Lace can be a little tricky to work with, but it is also very forgiving—your stitches do not need to be perfect. Use the glue pen to turn in hems and seams to prevent any fraying before you sew. If the lace has a finished edge—for example, if it is scalloped or perhaps pointed—then use that for the bottom of your gilet; it will look really pretty and will save you from having to sew a hem!

2 Place the back and front pieces right sides together and sew together at the shoulders. Turn in a hem around the armholes and stitch, then stitch down each side.

3 All that's left to do is to finish the two raw edges at the front of the gilet, turn in a small hem and stitch. Use a backstitch throughout and then go over the edge of any seam with a blanket stitch to prevent fraying.

tassel boots

1 Using the template on page 115, cut four tassel boot pieces from faux suede or felt.

2 Turn down a small hem at the top of each boot piece and backstitch. Now place two pieces right sides together and sew around the shoe, leaving the top open.

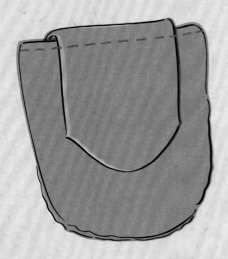

3 Cut out a tassel piece for each boot, leaving it whole for now (the tassels will be cut later). Fold the top over the edge of the boot and stitch in place, sewing in line with the existing stitches around the top of the shoe.

4 Using small embroidery scissors make small snips about three-quarters of the way up the tassel piece to make your faux suede tassels! Repeat steps 2–4 to make a second boot.

tassel bag

1 Using the templates on page 114, cut out all the bag pattern pieces from faux suede or felt. Turn a small hem at the top of the bag front to finish the raw edge.

2 Place the bag front piece and the back and flap piece right sides together and sew around the bottom of the bag.

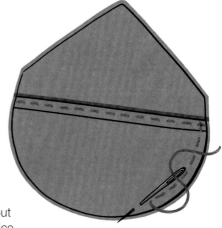

3 Turn the bag out the right way and push out the seams to get a nice clean curve.

4 Using the glue pen, turn a small hem around the bag flap and, at the same time, place the bag tassel piece underneath this hem and stitch around the turned edge of the flap. You can now cut the tassels in the same way as the shoes.

5 Cut a strip of fabric that is 8 x ½ in. (20 x 1 cm) for the bag strap (you can always make the strap longer or shorter). Fold both long raw edges in to the center, stitch along each side using a backstitch.

6 Use a few straight stitches to attach the strap to the left-hand side of the bag, then use a snap fastener to attach the other side of the strap—this means that you can open the bag strap for your doll to wear it cross body.

flower crown

1 Cut a strip measuring approx. 6 x ½ in. (15 x 1 cm) from green felt. This is the hairband base for your flower crown. Fold both long edges in to the center and use the glue pen to secure, pressing down firmly as you go. Then give a gentle tug along the hairband; it will thin out a bit, but also become quite strong and pliable. Measure it for fit from the left seam on your doll's hair to the opposite seam, then snip off any excess.

2 Using the flower templates on page 115 as a guide, cut out as many flowers and leaves as you like from scraps of colored felt. To make the rose, simply roll up the pattern piece and secure it with stitches underneath, keeping the base flat and passing your needle through all the layers at the base. You can also add a leaf or two to the base.

3 To make the poppy-style flower, cut out five petals, a base, and a center. Arrange the petals on the base and secure with the glue pen, then add the center of the flower on top and sew through all the layers to secure. Make a few more stitches in the center.

4 Play around with the placement of the flowers and leaves on the hairband, then attach them one by one by making a few random stitches at the back of each to secure to the hairband.

5 Add the flower crown to the doll's head using some discrete straight stitches at each end and in behind some of the flowers and leaves.

noah

This handsome sailor has just reached port and can't wait to see his beloved Ruby! He is smartly turned out in his best denims and soft, jersey-knit striped sweater. Noah's mustache is perfectly groomed and his hair expertly coiffed. Have fun with Noah's tattoos: maybe stitch a sweet message or a loved one's name.

you will need

Basic doll templates on page 110

Noah hair template on page 118

Noah templates on page 122

Skin-tone, brown, and black felt for the doll

Stranded embroidery floss (cotton) in assorted colors

Small amount of wool roving for the mustache

Denim fabric for the jeans

Small length of fine elastic

Striped jersey fabric for the sweater

Two or three snap fasteners

Faux suede for the boots (or some tan felt)

Glue pen

Basic sewing kit

noah's hair, face and tattoos

1 Using the Basic Doll templates and Noah's hair and eye templates, cut out all the pattern pieces. Add Noah's tattoos BEFORE the arms are sewn together, just don't stitch too close to the edge of the arm or you will lose detail when the arm is turned out the right way. I stitched an anchor, Ruby's name, and a tiny red felt heart with an arrow through it. Use one strand of embroidery thread, small straight stitches, and a fine needle

2 Continue to stitch and assemble the doll, following the instructions on page 12. Noah's face is slightly different and has a different eye shape from the girls. Attach Noah's hair following the instructions on page 13 and then stitch on Noah's eyes with a blanket stitch.

3 The hair flick and mustache are added at the end once the doll has been stuffed and assembled. A few straight stitches in the center of the mustache will fix it to the face. Cut out two hair flicks from brown felt and stick them together with the glue pen. Follow the sewing guides marked on the template to add some hair detail in backstitch.

4 Once the doll had been put together, attach the hair flick by sewing a line of stitching down the parting.

jeans

1 Using the template on page 122, cut two pattern pieces from denim fabric and place right sides together. Begin by sewing the inside leg seams and then snip into the tight curve at the top of the inner leg seams, this will give a nice smooth finish when turned out the right way.

2 Stitch down either side of the jeans and then turn ¼ in. (5 mm) over to the wrong side at the waist. Add elastic to the waist as you would to make doll pants (see page 16). Turn the jeans right way out, put them on your doll and then add turn-ups to the bottom of the jeans.

sweater

1 Using the templates on page 123, cut out one front and two back pieces from the striped jersey fabric. Turn in all hems at the neckline and down the center back, secure with a glue pen, and sew using backstitch.

2 Place the front and one back piece right sides together and sew across the shoulders and down the sleeves. Turn a small hem at the end of the sleeves and sew, then place the sweater right sides together again and sew up the sleeve to the underarm and down the side of the sweater; repeat for the other side.

3 Hem the bottom of the sweater and add two or three snap fasteners to the back.

boots

1 Using the template on page 122, cut four boot pattern pieces from faux suede (felt could also be used). Turn down a small hem at the top of each one and sew.

2 Place two boot pieces right sides together and sew around, leaving the top of the boot open. Turn out the right way and push out the seams to give a nice curve.

ruby

Ruby's delicate lace skirt and peach crop top are the height of summer fashion, perfectly accessorized with a quilted chain bag and a beautiful oversized blossom in her raven hair. A soft pastel color palette will work perfectly with pale lace.

you will need

- Basic doll templates on page 110
- Side-bun hair template on page 119
- Ruby templates on page 124
- Skin-tone, brown, and black felt for the doll
- Stranded embroidery floss (cotton) in assorted colors
- Cotton fabric for the pants and crop top
- Small length of fine elastic
- 14 x 3½ in. (35 x 9 cm) plain cotton fabric for the underskirt

- 14 x 3½ in. (35 x 9 cm) lace
- Navy felt for the shoes, bag, and flower center
- White and green felt for the flower and leaf
- Gold-colored chain for the bag handle
- ¼-in. (6-mm) button
- Two snap fasteners
- Glue pen
- Basic sewing kit

cutting out and making the doll

Using the templates for the Basic Doll and the Side-bun hair, cut out, stitch, and assemble the doll, following the instructions on page 12.

pants

Follow the instructions for the doll pants on page 16

crop top

Refer to Edie on page 87 to make a crop top from cotton fabric.

lace skirt

1 Lay the lace strip on top of the underskirt fabric strip. If there is a finished edge to your lace, use that for the hemline of your skirt; it will look really pretty and will also mean that you don't have to sew it!

2 Fold down approx. ¼ in. (5 mm) to the wrong side at the waistline. With the right side of the fabric facing you, sew a running stitch along the waist, gathering your fabrics every inch (2.5 cm) or so and taking a small backstitch just to secure the gathers.

3 Keep measuring against your doll's waist for fit—my doll's waist was 6 in. (15 cm), but yours may be a little more or less. When you have the desired length to fit around the waist, fold a small hem of both lace and cotton at each end.

4 Hem the cotton underskirt only, unless your lace is unfinished, in which case I would hem it separately from the underskirt.

5 Sew both hems at either end of the skirt. Attach the button to one of the top corners, then tie a small loop of fine elastic and stitch it to the opposite corner to fasten the lace skirt onto the doll. Alternatively, you could use a snap fastener instead of a button and loop

quilted bag

1 Using the templates on page 124, cut out all the bag pieces from navy felt and also cut 8 in.(20 cm) of gold-colored chain.

2 Add some detail to the felt by stitching some diagonal lines in backstitch to make the bag look quilted.

3 Using a whipstitch, attach the gusset to the front of the bag, going down one side, along the bottom, and up the other side.

4 Sew the bag back to the gusset in the same way, then fold the flap over the front of your bag and add a snap fastener, if needed, to close the bag. Attach some gold-colored chain to each side using a few small stitches and the bag is complete!

large hair flower

1 Using the templates on page 124, cut five petals from white felt, a center from navy felt, and a leaf from green felt. Also cut a small round scrap of felt for the base. Using some blusher and a cotton bud, blend in some color to the bottom portion of each petal.

2 Secure each petal to the scrap piece of felt with the glue pen. Then position the navy center on top and place the leaf underneath. Sew a few stitches through the center and around the flower center.

3 You could add some elastic here to make a hair tie, or perhaps even sew on a brooch back, I simply stitched the flower to Ruby's hair, using a ladder stitch in the same color thread as her hair.

shoes

Use the templates for the Basic Shoe on page 111 to cut out two soles and two uppers from navy felt. Follow the instructions on page 16 to complete the shoes.

olivia

Recreate Olivia's duffel coat, which is her favorite thing to wear, using felt and some tiny toggle buttons. She has teamed it with a delicate floral dress and a pretty little blossom in her top-knot. How stylish!

cutting out and making the doll

Using the templates for the Basic Doll and the Top-knot hair, cut out, stitch, and assemble the doll, following the instructions on page 12. Note that Olivia's hair goes over one eye, so you will need to sketch and stitch the eyes before attaching the hair.

dress

1 Cut a strip of cotton fabric that is 3½ x 20 in. (9 x 50 cm) and set aside—this will be for the skirt of the dress. Refer to Amber on page 21 to make a sleeveless bodice from the remaining cotton fabric. Because this is a sleeveless dress, you will need to snip right into the seam allowance around the armhole, then turn in and sew.

2 Take the strip of skirt fabric and fold and glue a small hem at the right-hand end. Place the bodice and the skirt right sides together with the bodice on top, lining up both edges at the top right-hand corner. Backstitch along the waistband, with approx. ⅛-in. (3-mm) seam allowance, folding small ¼-in. (5-mm) pleats as you go, with perhaps two or three stitches between each one. You may not need all 20 in. (50 cm) of fabric, depending on how many pleats you add (more pleats will give a fuller dress).

3 When you get to the far end, turn a small hem and secure with glue pen. Stitch the hem at each end of the skirt and turn a hem along the bottom, sewing with backstitch. Add two snap fasteners to the back of the bodice and two ⅛-in. (4-mm) buttons to cover them.

doll pants

Follow the instructions for the doll pants on page 16.

you will need

Basic doll templates on page 110

Top-knot hair template on page 119

Olivia, Amber, and Ruby templates on pages 121, 112, and 124

Skin-tone, brown, and black felt for the doll

Black, pink, brown, and white stranded embroidery floss (cotton)

20 x 10 in. (50 x 25 cm) cotton fabric for the dress

Two snap fasteners

Two ⅛-in. (4-mm) buttons

9 x 36 in. (23 x 90 cm) olive felt for the duffel coat

Three small toggle buttons

Pale pink and navy felt for flower

Small length of fine elastic

Pale blue felt for shoes

Glue pen

Basic sewing kit

duffel coat

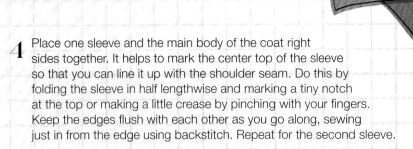

1 Using the templates on page 121, cut out all the duffel coat pieces from olive felt.

2 Place the back and one front coat piece right sides together and sew along the shoulder seam. Repeat for the second front piece.

3 Next add the sleeves. As you are using felt, there is no need for a seam allowance or to snip into the curve—there is enough "give" in the felt to ensure a nice clean curve.

4 Place one sleeve and the main body of the coat right sides together. It helps to mark the center top of the sleeve so that you can line it up with the shoulder seam. Do this by folding the sleeve in half lengthwise and marking a tiny notch at the top or making a little crease by pinching with your fingers. Keep the edges flush with each other as you go along, sewing just in from the edge using backstitch. Repeat for the second sleeve.

5 When you have added both sleeves, fold one sleeve so that it is right sides together and stitch from the "cuff" to the underarm and from the underarm down the side of the coat. Repeat for the other side and turn out the right way.

6 Now turn in and stitch a hem down either side of the front of the coat.

7 Now work on the hood by stitching one hood piece to the center hood panel. Do this using the same technique you did for the sleeve, stitching just in from the edge. Repeat with the other half of the hood and then turn out the right way. You may have to trim the central hood panel at this point, if there is any excess left.

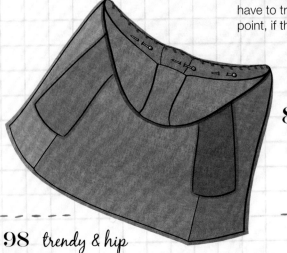

8 Place the hood and coat right sides together and pin in place, then simply whipstitch around the edge. Keep your stitches small and close together, using a similar-colored thread to the coat, and you will barely see the stitches.

9 Now all that's left to do are the details. Cut two pocket shapes from olive felt and stitch a narrow hem across the top of each one. Sew the pockets to the coat, going down one side, around the bottom, and up the other side.

10 Add the three toggle buttons down the left front. Using some small embroidery scissors, make small snips into the right front for buttonholes. Start off small—don't be tempted to make large cuts.

11 Finish the coat by sewing a blanket stitch around the bottom edge and the top of the hood to finish off the edges.

hair flower

1 Using the Ruby templates on page 124, cut five petals, two leaf shapes, and a flower center from felt. You'll also need to cut a small scrap piece of felt for the base.

2 Using the glue pen, stick the petals to the base piece of felt, pressing down as you go with the end of a pencil or pen to add strength. Add the flower center to the top. Make a few stitches through the center to secure it and then sew some random straight stiches with a little French knot at the ends, working all around the flower.

3 Turn the flower over and lay a piece of elastic across the back. Position the leaves over the elastic and secure with a glue pen and/or a few stitches.

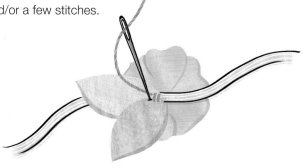

shoes

Use the templates for the Pointy Shoe on page 111 to cut out two soles and two uppers from pale blue felt. Follow the instructions on page 16 to complete the shoes.

4 Tie the ends of the elastic and trim—you now have a miniature hair bobble to tie around your doll's top-knot hair bun.

isla

Isla is off for a brisk autumnal walk through the woods. She loves to forage for blackberries, apples, and elderberries. Once her basket is laden with fruit, she will head back home to bake something yummy with her loot. She's a bit of a whizz in the kitchen. Her mustard yellow cape will keep her warm as she trudges through the forest.

you will need

Basic doll templates on page 110

Cute bob hair template on page 119

Isla and Kayla templates on page 120

Skin-tone, brown, and black felt for the doll

Stranded embroidery floss (cotton) in assorted colors

Cotton fabric for the dress and doll pants

Three snap fasteners

Mustard yellow felt for the cape

Two 1/8-in. (4-mm) buttons

Navy felt for the basket and shoes

Scrap of gingham fabric for the basket

Scrap of fabric for the bow

Washable fabric marker

Glue pen

Basic sewing kit

cutting out and making the doll

Using the templates for the Basic Doll and the Cute Bob hair, cut out, stitch, and assemble the doll, following the instructions on page 12.

dress

Follow the instructions on page 107 for Kayla's floaty-sleeved dress.

doll pants

Follow the instructions for the doll pants on page 16.

shoes

Use the templates for the Basic Shoe on page 111 to cut out two soles and two uppers from navy felt. Follow the instructions on page 16 to complete the shoes.

cape

1 Using the templates on page 120, cut out one back, two fronts, two collar fronts, one collar back, and one collar strap from mustard yellow felt.

2 Place the cape back and one cape front piece right sides together. Starting at the neckline and using a backstitch, sew along the shoulder and down the side. Repeat to add the second cape front piece to the other side.

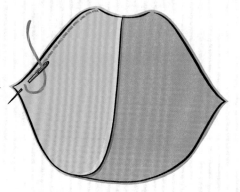

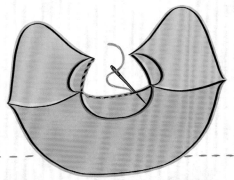

3 Turn the cape out the right way and attach the collar pieces, using a whipstitch in a matching color of thread.

4 Using a running stitch (or alternatively you could use a blanket stitch), sew all around the edges of the cape, including around the collar pieces.

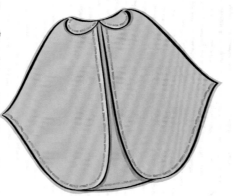

5 Take your strap piece; if your felt feels very thin, then cut out an extra piece and stack them on top of each other, but if your felt seems sturdy enough then just use one piece.

6 Sew around the strap using a backstitch; this is for both decoration and to add strength to such a small piece of felt.

7 Lay the cape flat and put the strap in place, making sure that it is lined up straight. Draw around the pointed ends with the fabric pen to make a really helpful guideline.

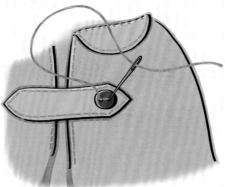

8 Stitch one side of the strap to the cape front, adding a button as you do so.

9 Add the top half of the snap fastener to the underside of the other end of the strap, with a button on top. Then add the bottom half of the snap fastener to the cape front, using the guidelines to help with placement.

basket

1 Use the basket template to draw around the shape on a piece of navy felt that is at least double the size of the template. Flip the template over and draw around it again so that the handle is extended and you now have one pattern piece. Draw around the base too and cut both pieces out.

2 Draw some criss-cross diagonal lines onto the main body of the basket and stitch over them using a running stitch to give a "basket" texture.

3 Fold the piece in half, right sides together, and sew down each side of the basket.

4 Add the base using a whipstitch in a matching color thread. Begin at one of the basket side seams and line up the base edge with the bottom edge of the basket, lining it up every ½ in. (1 cm) or so.

5 Turn right side out. The basket is now complete, but to give it a nice finish, run a small blanket stitch around the rim and the handle. Finally, cut a 3-in. (8-cm) square of gingham to put in the basket.

bow

1 Cut one strip that is 4 x 1½ in. (10 x 4 cm) and a smaller strip that is 1½ x ¾ in. (4 x 2 cm) from your cotton fabric.

2 Fold the long raw edges of both strips in to the center and secure with glue pen.

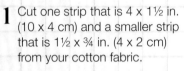

3 Fold the ends of the larger strip in to the center and secure with glue pen.

4 Wrap the center strip around the middle of the bow. It might be helpful to pinch the bow in the middle with your fingers first, then wrap the center strip around. The strip will be longer than you need, but the extra length makes it easier to handle. Secure with the glue pen, then trim off any excess. Add a few stitches to fix in place and, without cutting the thread, attach to the dolls head. Stitch through the doll's hair first, then into the back of the bow. Pull gently to tighten and bring the bow flush with the head. Repeat until the bow feels secure.

heidi

Heidi is a riot of bright cheery color, much like her sweet personality. Her Liberty of London print dress and glitter shoes perfectly complement her candy pink hair. Larger than the other dolls and with a body made from cotton, she would make the perfect gift.

you will need

Basic doll templates on page 110

Side-swept hair template on page 118

Amber and Kayla templates on pages 112 and 120

Skin-tone cotton for the body

Stranded embroidery floss (cotton) in assorted colors

Pink felt for the hair

Black felt for the eyes

Floral print cotton for the dress

Contrast cotton for the pants

Small length of fine elastic

Glitter fabric for the shoes

Small piece of white felt for the placket

Three ¼-in. (6-mm) buttons

Two snap fasteners

Washable fabric marker

Glue pen

Basic sewing kit

cutting out and making the doll

To make this larger size doll you will need to enlarge the templates for the Basic Doll by 180% and the Side-swept hair by 380% to create a doll that is approximately 24 in. (60 cm) tall. Use these templates to cut the body, head, neck, arms, and legs from skin-tone cotton. Cut the hair from pink felt.

face and body

1 Heidi's body, face, and head are put together in the same way as the smaller felt dolls. However, instead of stitching close to the edge as you would with felt, use a ¼-in. (5-mm) seam allowance on the limbs and the body. This will guard against fraying, which cotton would have a tendency to do if the seam were too close to the edge. The result of a larger seam allowance is nice strong seams that hold the toy stuffing well. Use the fabric marker and a ruler to mark the ¼-in. (5-mm) seams on any straight edges of the pattern pieces, such as the limbs and the body back, then draw any curves by hand.

2 Following the instructions for the Basic Doll on page 12, continue to make the body and limbs.

3 Heidi's hair is made from felt like all the other dolls, so a smaller seam allowance will be fine here, but use the fabric pen to draw a slightly larger seam allowance where the hair is stitched to the cotton neck. Follow the instructions on page 13 to finish the face and hair.

doll pants

Enlarge the doll pants templates by 180%, as before, and use them to cut the pattern pieces from your cotton fabric. Follow the instructions on page 16 to complete the pants.

dress

Follow the instructions for Kayla's dress on page 107 to make a dress for Heidi, remembering that you will need to enlarge the pattern pieces for the sleeveless bodice and sleeve by 180% before you cut them out. Cut a piece of white felt for the placket, using scalloped scissors if you have them. Attach to the front of the dress using glue pen, then stitch on three decorative buttons to finish.

shoes

Enlarge the Basic Shoe template on page 111 by 180% and use to cut two soles and two uppers from glitter fabric. It is probably worth checking the size against your finished doll's foot to make sure it will be a snug fit. Follow the instructions on page 16 to complete both shoes.

tips for sewing glitter shoes

❖ When making glitter shoes it isn't necessary to sew around the aperture in the front of the shoe. The glue in the fabric (that keeps the glitter stuck to the fabric) makes it quite resilient to fraying.

❖ Use a fine needle and strong thread, as a thick needle would make it very difficult to sew—especially if the glitter fabric has chunky sequins on it.

❖ Draw a line to follow on the wrong side of the shoe upper. Your stitching does not need to be perfect—just make sure that your needle and thread go through this line as often as you can. Avoid large stitches and you will get a nice curve when the shoe is turned out the right way.

kayla

Kayla's pretty floaty-sleeved dress is really versatile, and worth learning to make—this bodice and skirt combo is the basis for other blouses and designs throughout the book. You could make lots of different looks from this one dress pattern: use a ditzy Liberty print with crochet trim, just like Kayla's, or contrasting fabrics, such as denim with stripes or polka dots, perhaps some corduroy or jersey knit. Trim with lace or mini pom-poms or even match the sleeves and the skirt and add a contrasting bodice!

you will need

Basic doll templates on page 110

Vintage waves hair template on page 118

Amber and Kayla templates on pages 112 and 120

Skin-tone, red, and black felt for the doll

Stranded embroidery floss (cotton) in assorted colors

Cotton fabric for the pants

Small length of fine elastic

Liberty print cotton for the dress

Crochet lace trim

Felt for the rose, shoes, and name tag

Two snap fasteners

Three flat-back pearls or ⅛-in. (4-mm) buttons or beads

Washable fabric marker

Glue pen

Basic sewing kit

cutting out and making the doll

Using the templates for the Basic Doll and the Vintage Waves hair, cut out, stitch, and assemble the doll, following the instructions on page 12. Make a rose for Kayla's hair by referring to the instructions for Edie's rose on page 89, step 2, making the rose a bit larger by adding a few extra petals.

doll pants

Follow the instructions for the doll pants on page 16.

dress

1 Using Amber's cami-top templates on page 112, cut out one cami-top front and two cami-top backs from your Liberty print cotton. Using the Kayla template on page 120, cut two sleeves.

2 Snip into the curved seam allowances at the neckline on all the cami-top pieces. Turn in and secure with glue pen. Turn in the straight hems at the center back pieces and fix with glue pen also. There is no need to snip or turn in the seam allowances at the armholes.

3 Sew these hems using a backstitch. You could use matching or a contrasting thread.

4 Place the front piece and one back piece right sides together and sew along the shoulder—this should only take two or three stitches. Repeat for the other back piece.

5 Mark the top center of the sleeves by folding them in half widthwise and pinching to make a small crease or mark with a fabric marker.

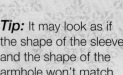

6 Place the sleeve and cami-top right sides together. Use a backstitch to start sewing the sleeve into the armhole. The size and shape of the sleeve allows for three pleats one on either side of the shoulder seam and one in the center to line up with the shoulder seam. Use the center mark on the sleeve to help with pleat placement. Repeat for the other sleeve.

Tip: It may look as if the shape of the sleeve and the shape of the armhole won't match up or fit together, but don't worry—just line up the edges every inch (2–3 cm) or so and stitch. This is called "easing in."

7 Finish the sleeves by turning under a small hem. There may only be a tiny space to do this at each end of the sleeve. If so, just fold under a sliver of fabric across the edge of the sleeve. Add the crochet lace trim to the underside of the sleeve as you backstitch this hem.

8 Place the cami-top back and front right sides together again and sew down the side seams; this will only be a few stitches.

9 Cut a strip of fabric about 4 x 15 in. (10 x 38 cm) for the skirt. Fold a hem at one end of the fabric and secure with glue pen, but don't sew. Place the skirt and top right sides together and stitch together, adding pleats as you go.

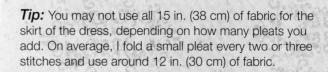

Tip: You may not use all 15 in. (38 cm) of fabric for the skirt of the dress, depending on how many pleats you add. On average, I fold a small pleat every two or three stitches and use around 12 in. (30 cm) of fabric.

10 Trim any excess fabric from the length, leaving ¼ in. (5 mm) for the hem. Turn this under and secure with glue pen. Finish all the hems using a backstitch. Sew a small hem along the bottom of the dress, adding the crochet lace trim as you go.

11 Add two snap fasteners to the back of the top and three flat back-pearls to the front of the dress with a little bit of fabric glue. Alternatively, you could use ⅛-in. (4-mm) buttons or some beads.

shoes

Use the Pointy Shoe templates on page 111 to cut out two soles and two uppers from green felt. Follow the instructions on page 16 to complete the shoes.

templates

Each template is clearly marked at the percentage of actual size it is printed. If a template is not at 100% it will need to be enlarged, templates printed at 50% will need to be enlarged by 200%, and those printed at 25% by 400%. You can do this using a photocopier. All the templates state clearly how many pieces you need to cut. Many items, such as bodices and skirts, have two back or two front pieces (or a left and a right piece). In these cases only one template is provided as the left and right pieces are exactly the same. All you need to do is cut two pieces, remembering to flip the template over if your fabric has a right and wrong side. See page 10 for more tips on using templates.

basic doll

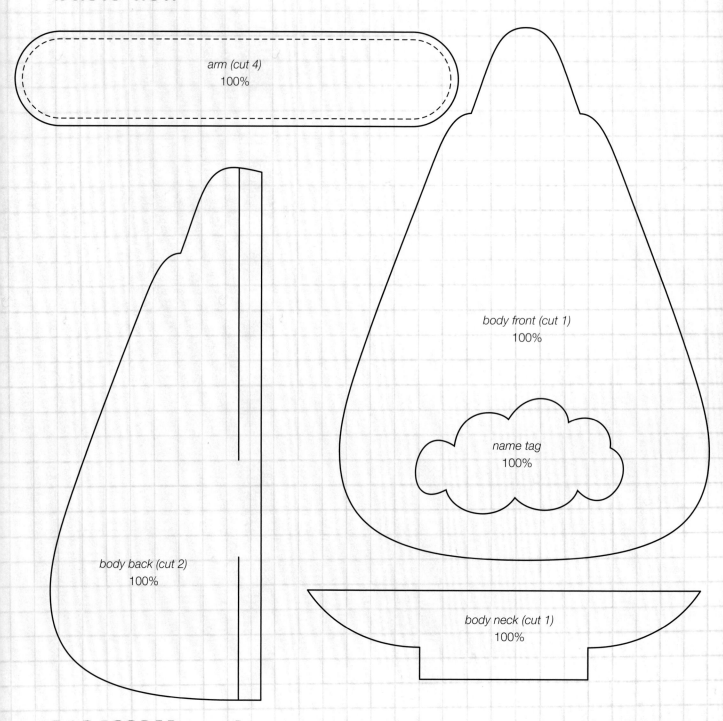

arm (cut 4)
100%

body front (cut 1)
100%

name tag
100%

body back (cut 2)
100%

body neck (cut 1)
100%

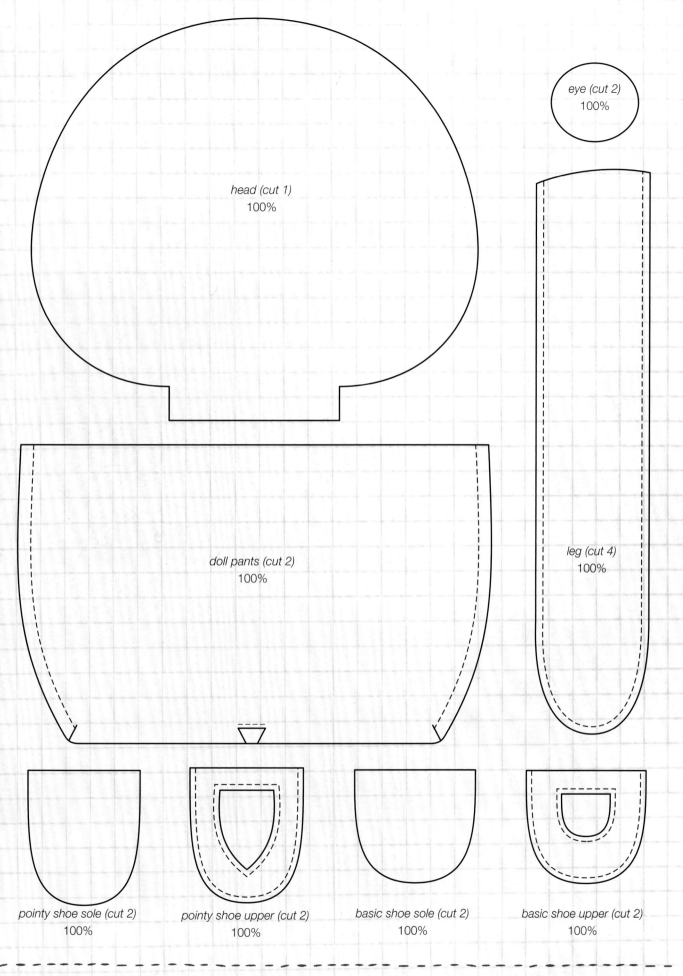

eye (cut 2)
100%

head (cut 1)
100%

leg (cut 4)
100%

doll pants (cut 2)
100%

pointy shoe sole (cut 2)
100%

pointy shoe upper (cut 2)
100%

basic shoe sole (cut 2)
100%

basic shoe upper (cut 2)
100%

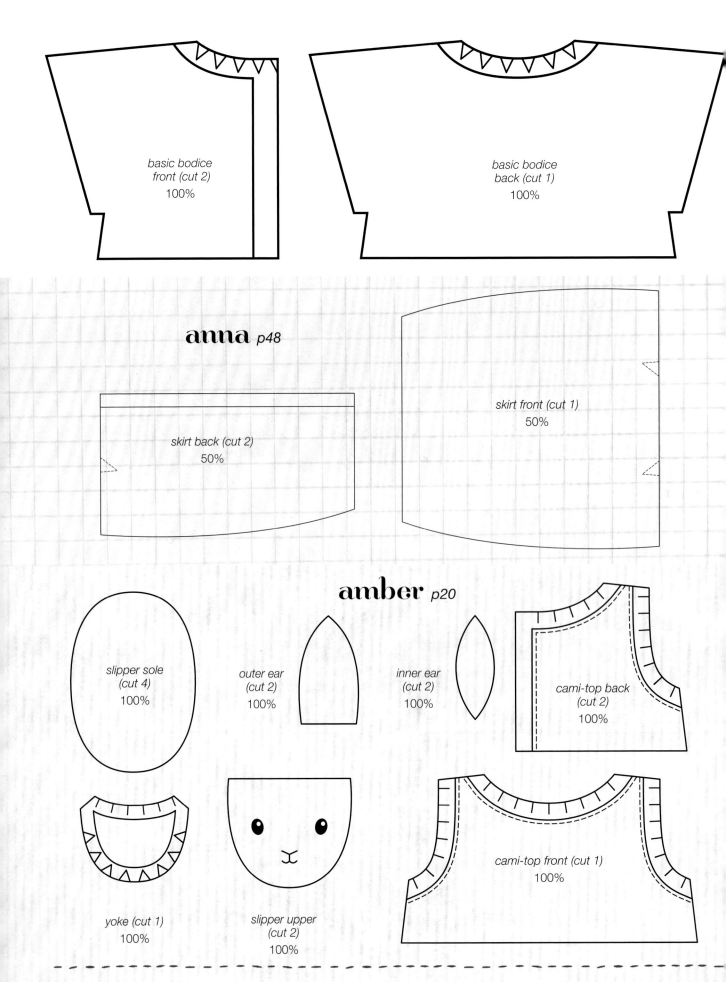

basic bodice
front (cut 2)
100%

basic bodice
back (cut 1)
100%

anna *p48*

skirt front (cut 1)
50%

skirt back (cut 2)
50%

amber *p20*

slipper sole
(cut 4)
100%

outer ear
(cut 2)
100%

inner ear
(cut 2)
100%

cami-top back
(cut 2)
100%

yoke (cut 1)
100%

slipper upper
(cut 2)
100%

cami-top front (cut 1)
100%

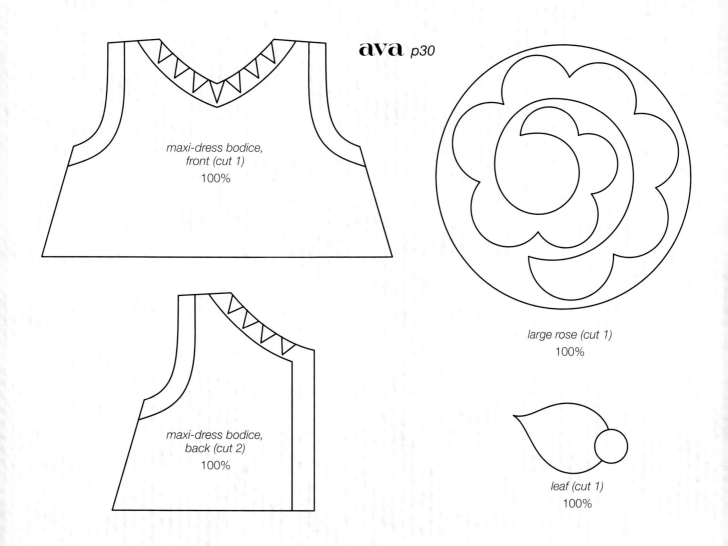

ava p30

maxi-dress bodice,
front (cut 1)
100%

large rose (cut 1)
100%

maxi-dress bodice,
back (cut 2)
100%

leaf (cut 1)
100%

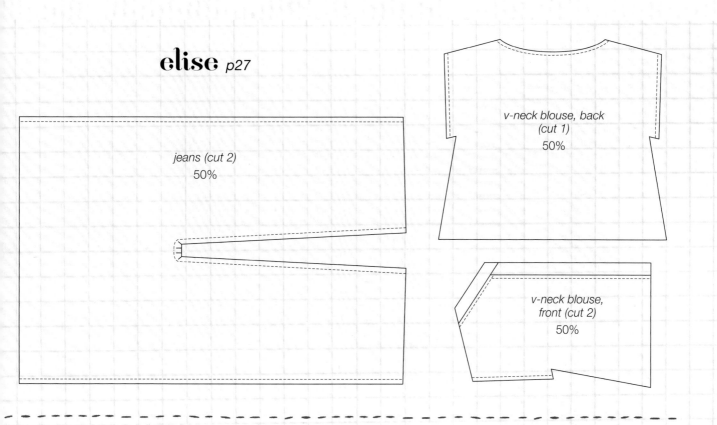

elise *p27*

jeans (cut 2)
50%

v-neck blouse, back
(cut 1)
50%

v-neck blouse,
front (cut 2)
50%

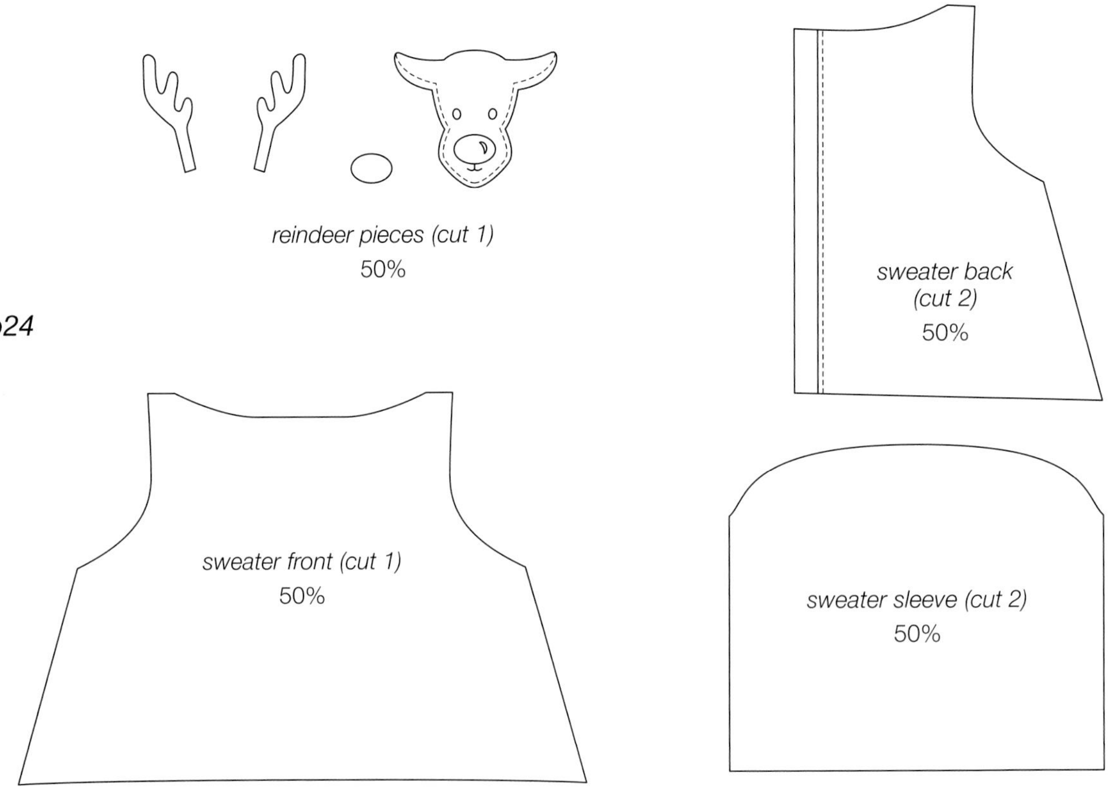

reindeer pieces (cut 1)
50%

chloe p24

sweater back
(cut 2)
50%

sweater front (cut 1)
50%

sweater sleeve (cut 2)
50%

edie p86

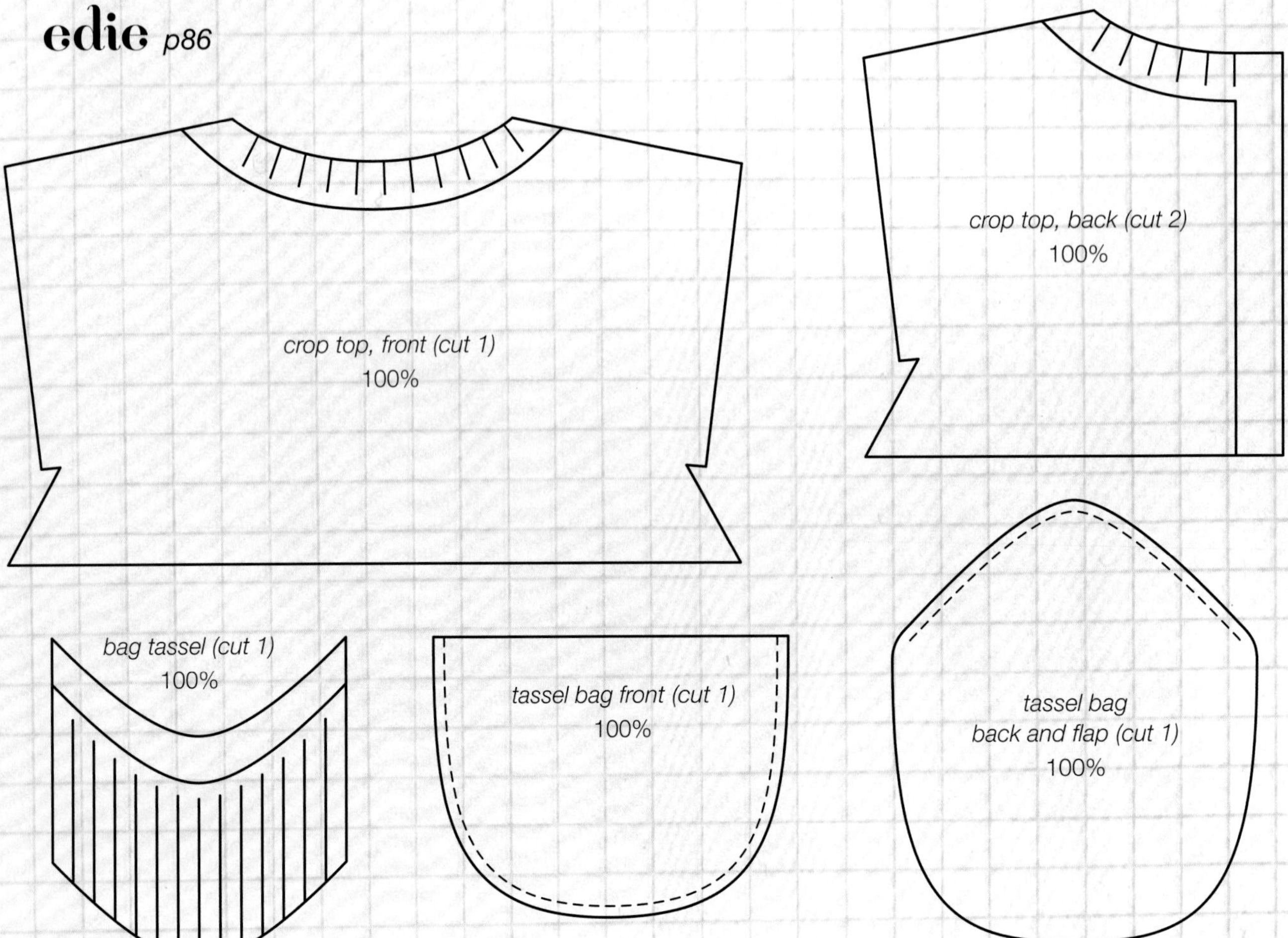

crop top, back (cut 2)
100%

crop top, front (cut 1)
100%

bag tassel (cut 1)
100%

tassel bag front (cut 1)
100%

tassel bag
back and flap (cut 1)
100%

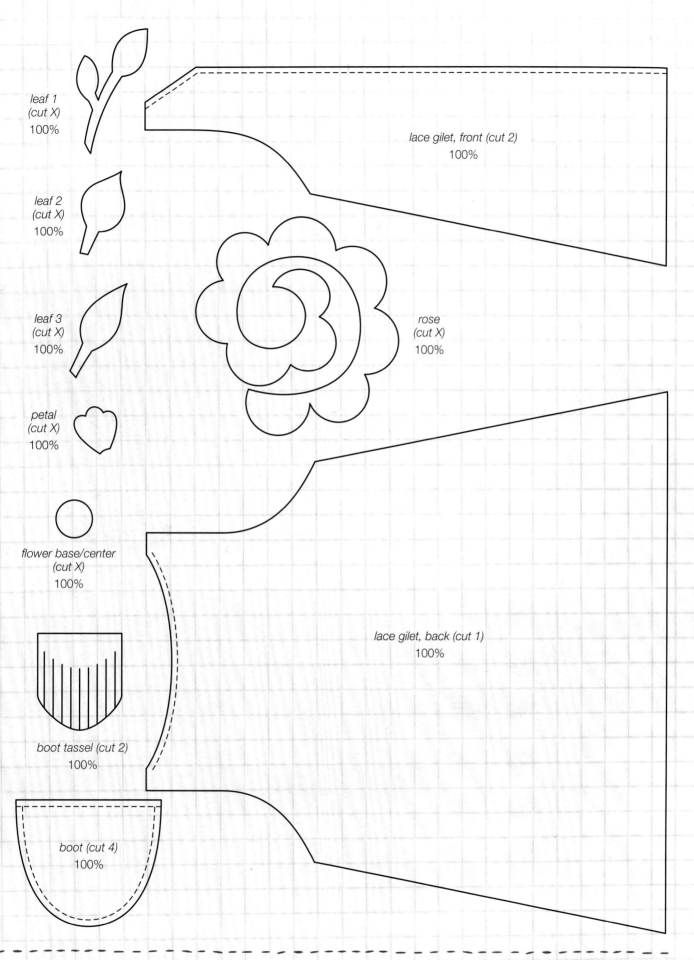

leaf 1
(cut X)
100%

leaf 2
(cut X)
100%

leaf 3
(cut X)
100%

petal
(cut X)
100%

flower base/center
(cut X)
100%

boot tassel (cut 2)
100%

boot (cut 4)
100%

lace gilet, front (cut 2)
100%

rose
(cut X)
100%

lace gilet, back (cut 1)
100%

girl squad *p70*

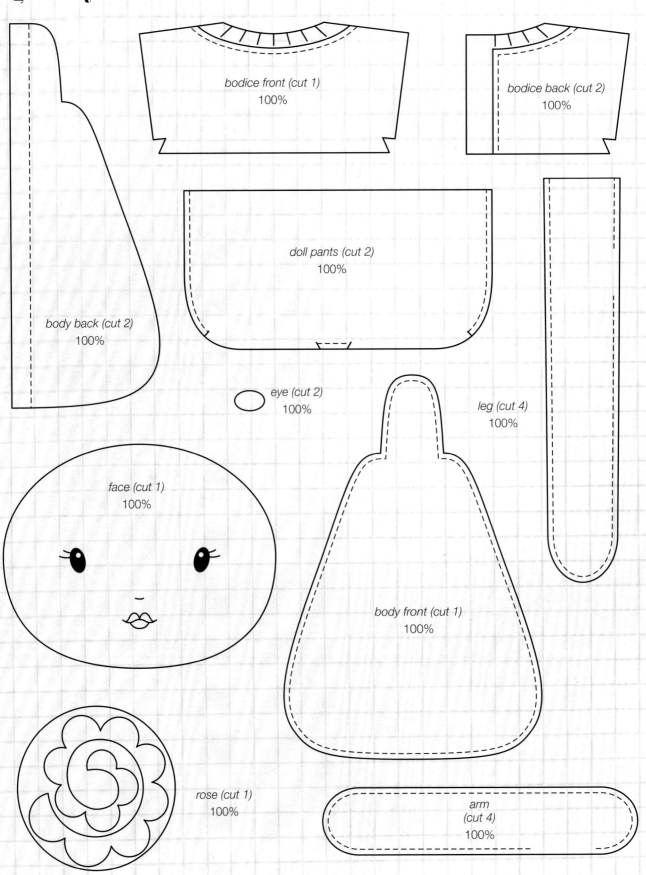

bodice front (cut 1)
100%

bodice back (cut 2)
100%

doll pants (cut 2)
100%

body back (cut 2)
100%

eye (cut 2)
100%

leg (cut 4)
100%

face (cut 1)
100%

body front (cut 1)
100%

rose (cut 1)
100%

arm
(cut 4)
100%

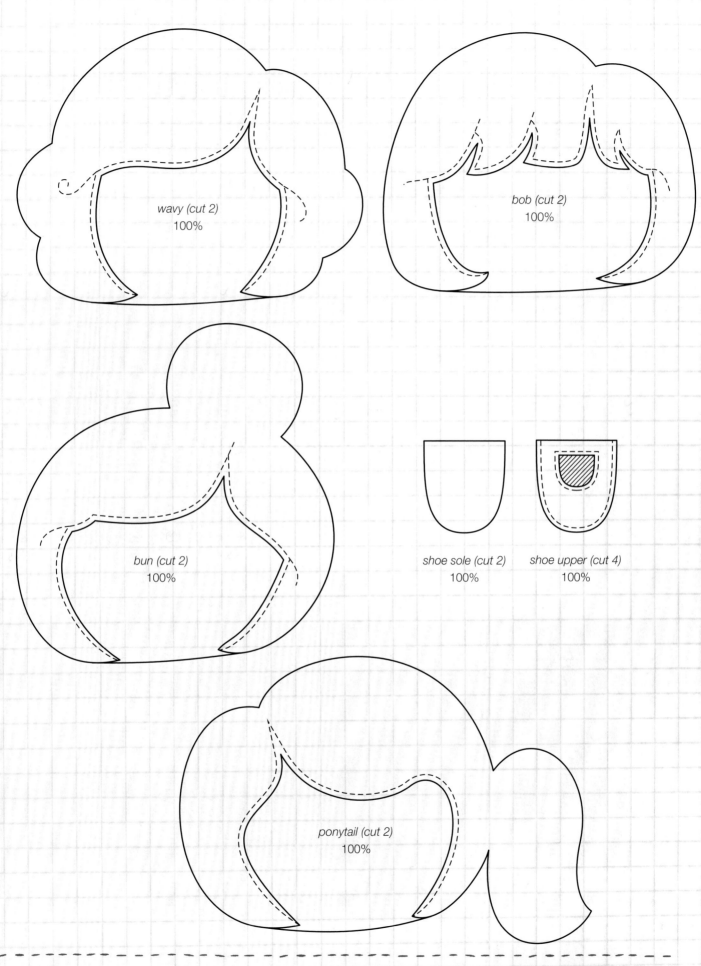

wavy (cut 2)
100%

bob (cut 2)
100%

bun (cut 2)
100%

shoe sole (cut 2)
100%

shoe upper (cut 4)
100%

ponytail (cut 2)
100%

hairstyles

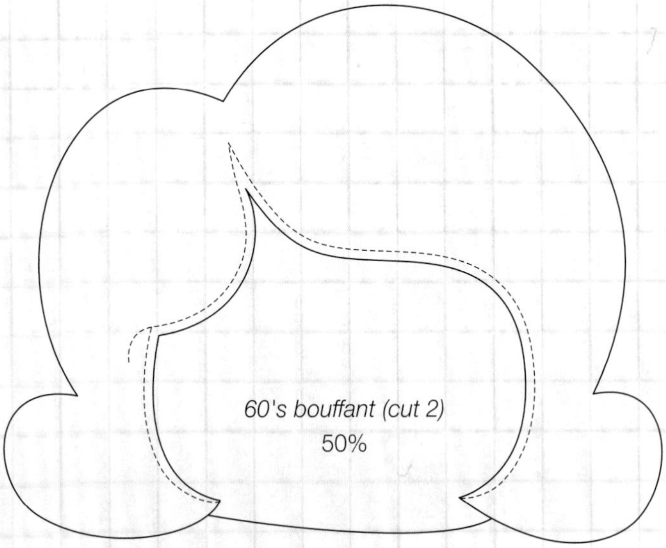

60's bouffant (cut 2)
50%

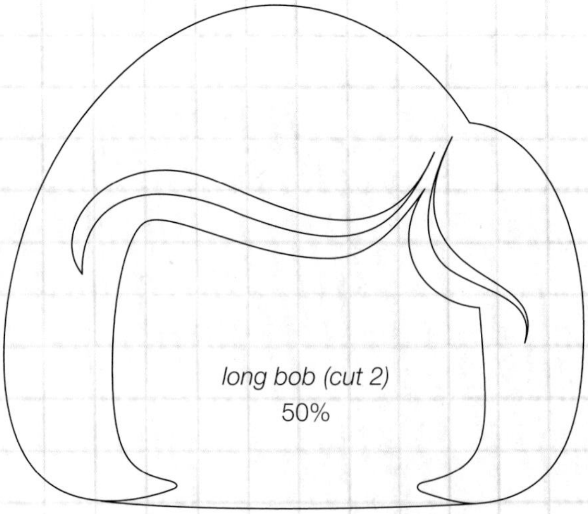

long bob (cut 2)
50%

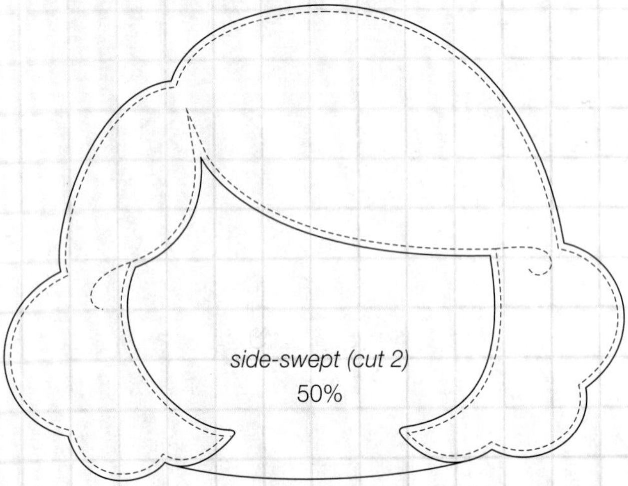

side-swept (cut 2)
50%

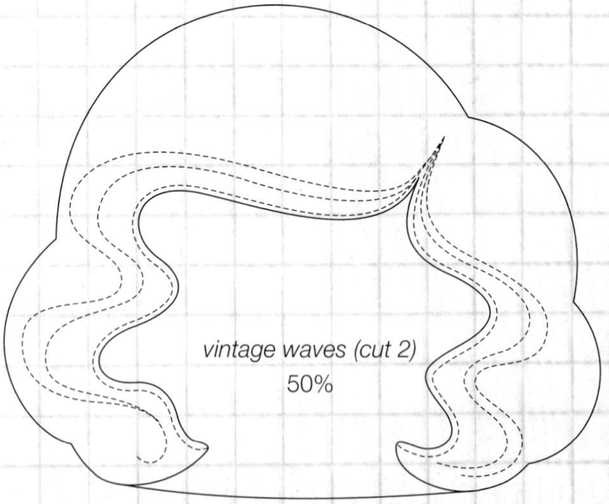

vintage waves (cut 2)
50%

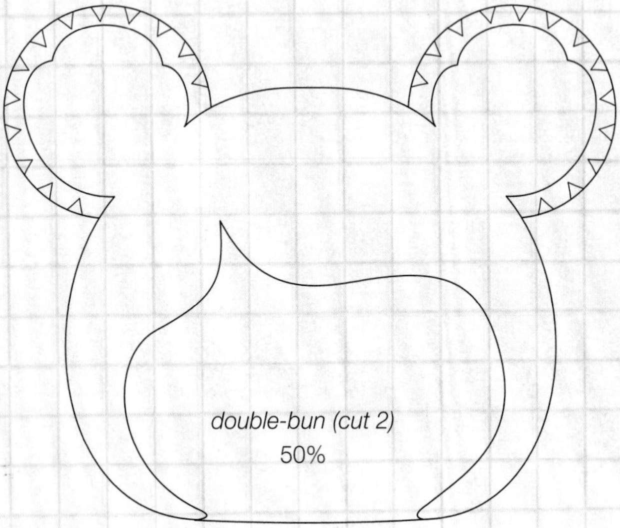

double-bun (cut 2)
50%

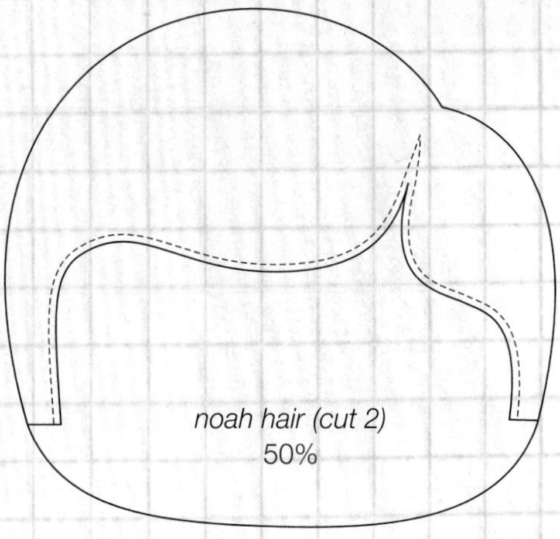

noah hair (cut 2)
50%

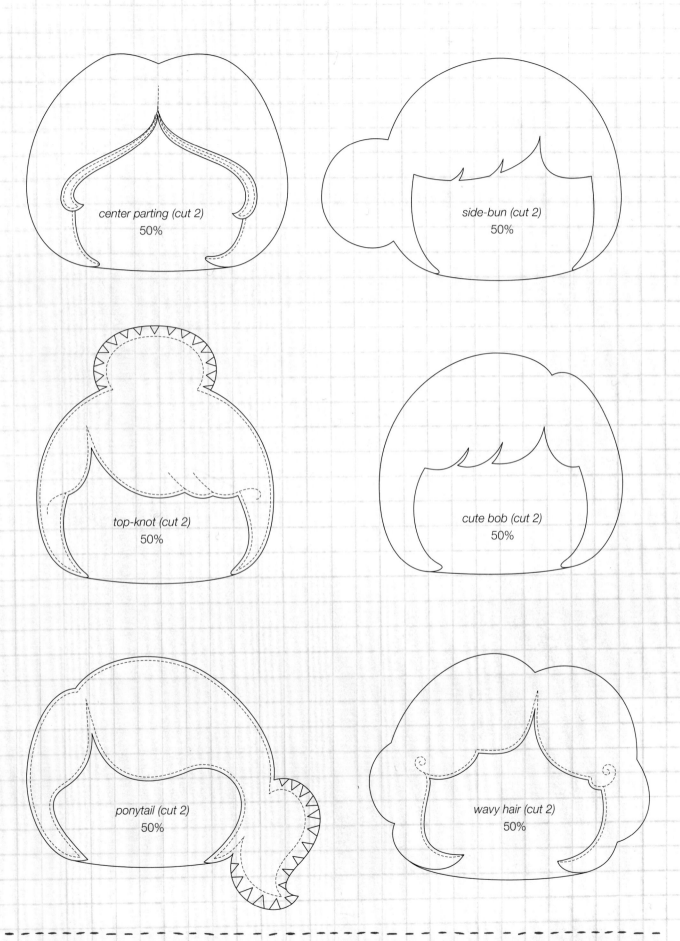

center parting (cut 2)
50%

side-bun (cut 2)
50%

top-knot (cut 2)
50%

cute bob (cut 2)
50%

ponytail (cut 2)
50%

wavy hair (cut 2)
50%

isla p100

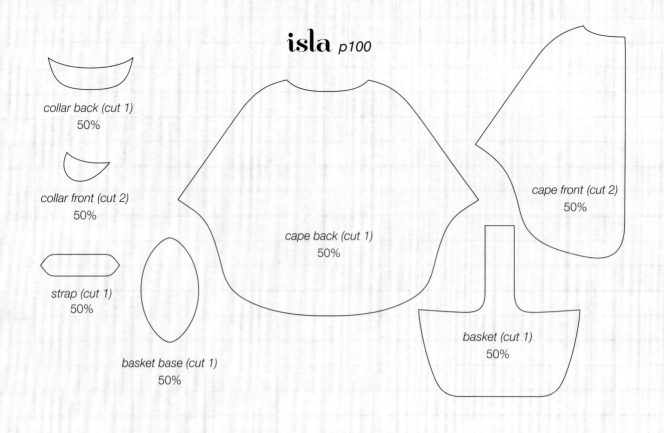

collar back (cut 1)
50%

collar front (cut 2)
50%

strap (cut 1)
50%

basket base (cut 1)
50%

cape back (cut 1)
50%

cape front (cut 2)
50%

basket (cut 1)
50%

kayla p107

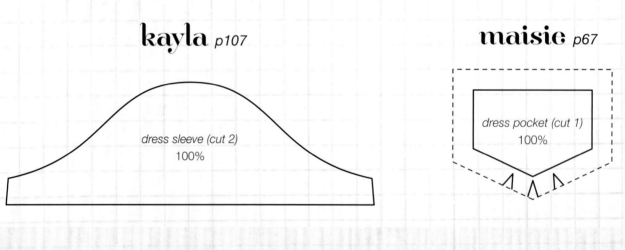

dress sleeve (cut 2)
100%

maisie p67

dress pocket (cut 1)
100%

lily p33

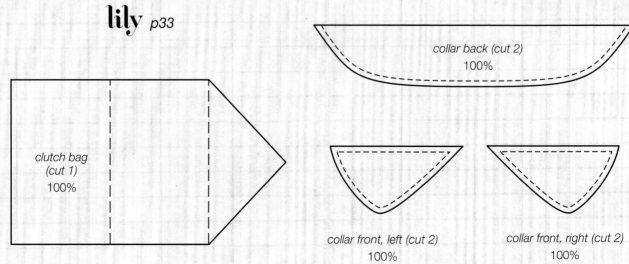

clutch bag
(cut 1)
100%

collar back (cut 2)
100%

collar front, left (cut 2)
100%

collar front, right (cut 2)
100%

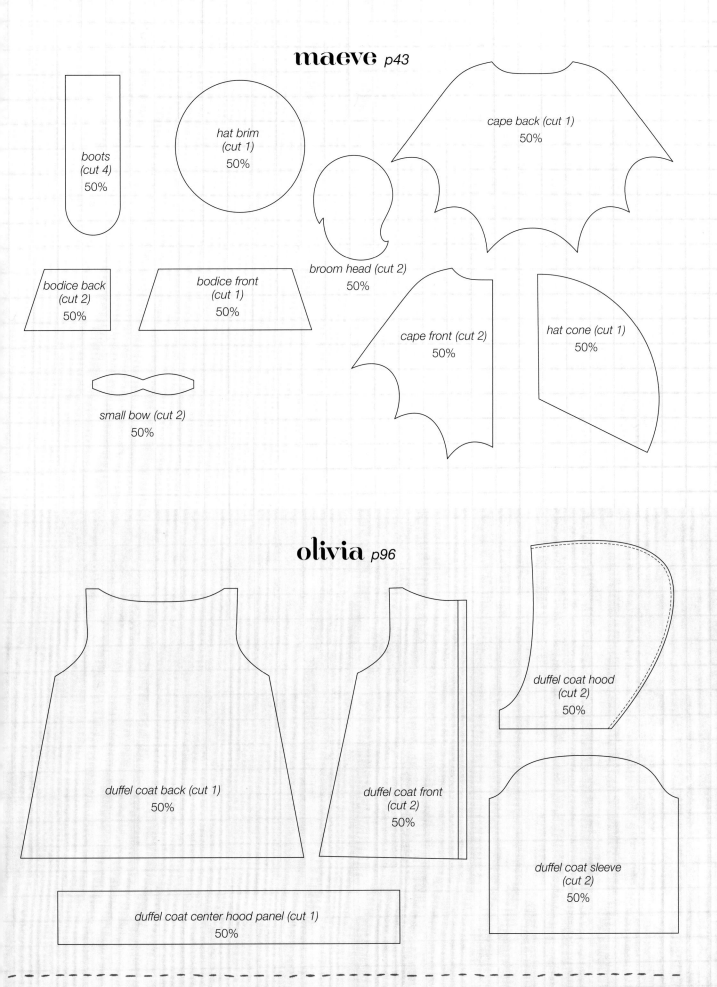

maeve *p43*

boots
(cut 4)
50%

hat brim
(cut 1)
50%

cape back (cut 1)
50%

broom head (cut 2)
50%

bodice back
(cut 2)
50%

bodice front
(cut 1)
50%

cape front (cut 2)
50%

hat cone (cut 1)
50%

small bow (cut 2)
50%

olivia *p96*

duffel coat hood
(cut 2)
50%

duffel coat back (cut 1)
50%

duffel coat front
(cut 2)
50%

duffel coat sleeve
(cut 2)
50%

duffel coat center hood panel (cut 1)
50%

mia *p36*

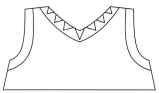

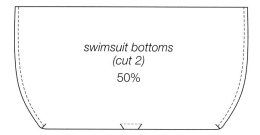

swimsuit bottoms
(cut 2)
50%

swimsuit top, back
(cut 1)
50%

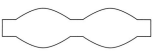

swimsuit top, front
(cut 2)
50%

flip-flop toe post (cut 2)
50%

starfish (cut 2)
50%

bow (cut 1)
50%

shell (cut 2)
50%

flip-flop sole (cut 4)
50%

bow band (cut 1)
50%

gingham shirt, back
(cut 1)
50%

gingham shirt, sleeve
(cut 2)
50%

noah *p90*

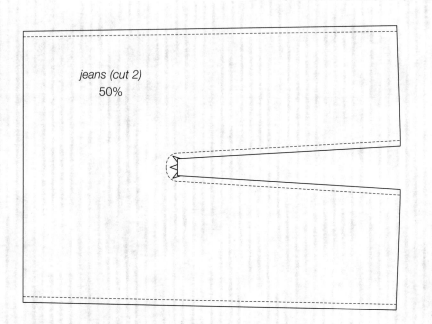

jeans (cut 2)
50%

boot (cut 4)
50%

eye (cut 2)
50%

penny *p56*

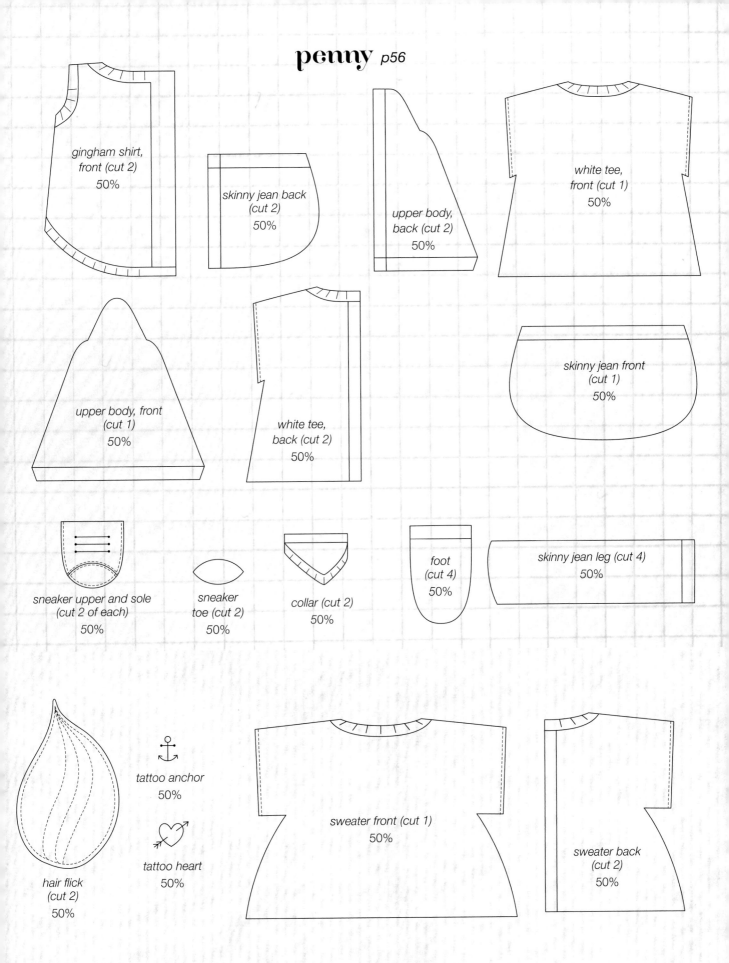

gingham shirt,
front (cut 2)
50%

skinny jean back
(cut 2)
50%

upper body,
back (cut 2)
50%

white tee,
front (cut 1)
50%

upper body, front
(cut 1)
50%

white tee,
back (cut 2)
50%

skinny jean front
(cut 1)
50%

sneaker upper and sole
(cut 2 of each)
50%

sneaker
toe (cut 2)
50%

collar (cut 2)
50%

foot
(cut 4)
50%

skinny jean leg (cut 4)
50%

hair flick
(cut 2)
50%

tattoo anchor
50%

tattoo heart
50%

sweater front (cut 1)
50%

sweater back
(cut 2)
50%

robyn *p64*

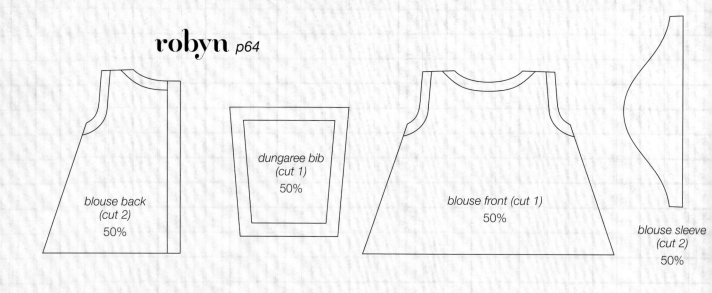

blouse back
(cut 2)
50%

dungaree bib
(cut 1)
50%

blouse front (cut 1)
50%

blouse sleeve
(cut 2)
50%

hannah *p40*

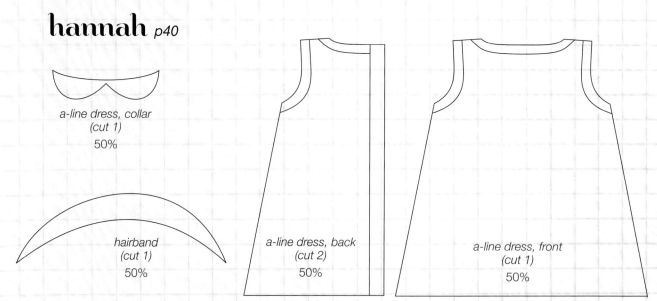

a-line dress, collar
(cut 1)
50%

hairband
(cut 1)
50%

a-line dress, back
(cut 2)
50%

a-line dress, front
(cut 1)
50%

ruby *p93*

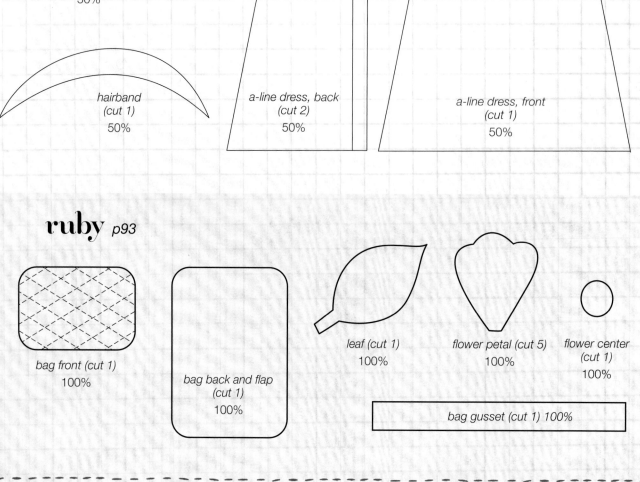

bag front (cut 1)
100%

bag back and flap
(cut 1)
100%

leaf (cut 1)
100%

flower petal (cut 5)
100%

flower center
(cut 1)
100%

bag gusset (cut 1) 100%

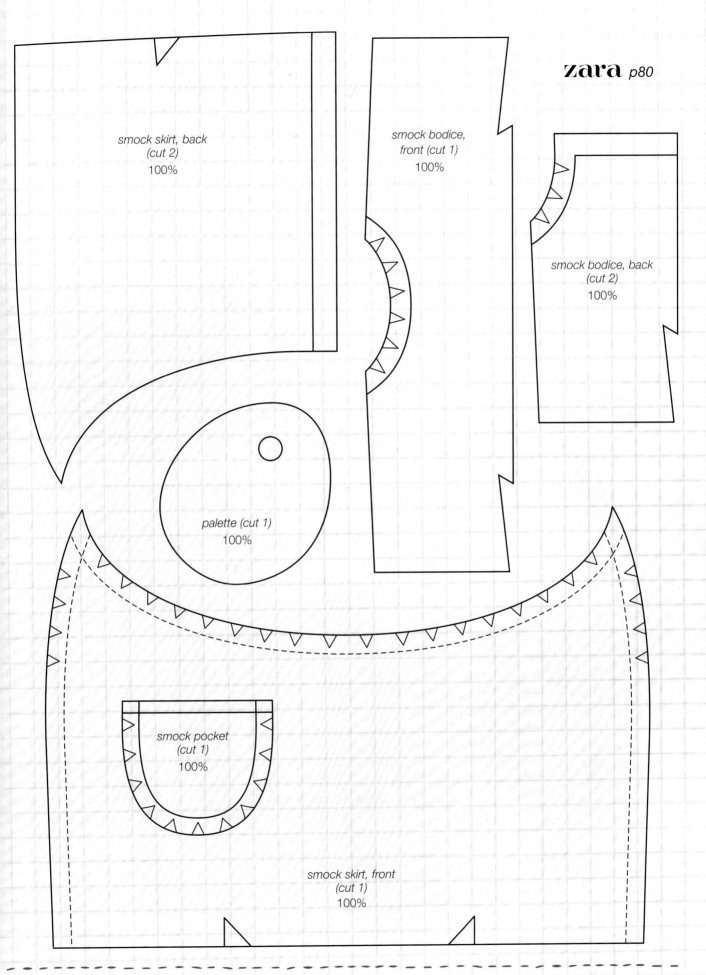

smock skirt, back
(cut 2)
100%

smock bodice,
front (cut 1)
100%

smock bodice, back
(cut 2)
100%

palette (cut 1)
100%

smock pocket
(cut 1)
100%

smock skirt, front
(cut 1)
100%

suppliers

US STOCKISTS

A.C. MOORE
www.hobbylobby.com

HOBBY LOBBY
www.hobbylobby.com

JO-ANN CRAFT STORE
www.joann.com

MICHAELS
www.michaels.com

UK STOCKISTS

ALICE CAROLINE
www.alicecaroline.co.uk
Liberty of London prints galore!

APPLE TREE CRAFTS
www.apletreecrafts.ie
Cute and dainty cotton prints.

BILLOW FABRICS
www.billowfabrics.co.uk
Wool mix felt in an amazing
selection of colors. Lovely quality.

CLOUD CRAFT
www.cloudcraft.co.uk
100% wool felt and matching DMC
threads.

COOL CRAFTING
www.coolcrafting.co.uk
Felt in unusual colors, notions,
ribbons, trims, cotton prints.

DUNELM
www.dunelm.com
Toy stuffing and Anchor threads.

ETERNAL MAKER
www.eternalmaker.com
Modern, edgy prints. Cotton, jersey,
corduroy, denim and all sorts of
dressmaking fabrics.

HOBBYCRAFT
www.hobbycraft.co.uk

JOHN LEWIS
www.johnlewis.com

PAPER AND STRING
www.paper-and-string.net
Wool mix felt, buttons and trims,
glitter fabric, and faux suede.

PIN IT AND STITCH
www.pinitandstitch.co.uk
Bright and modern cotton prints.

SIMPLY SOLIDS
www.simplysolids.co.uk
Kona cotton fabric (for skin tone
colors), cotton prints, Cosmo
embroidery floss.

VILENE
www.vlieseline.com
Vilene products, like Stitch and Tear
and toy stuffing.

index

acknowledgments

I would like to thank the following people; you all made this whole book thing a reality!

Thanks Mum and Dad, and my brother too, for walking the dogs for me and making me endless cups of tea. Your support and encouragement are priceless.

My dear friends Margaret and Laura—without a doubt, this book is a direct result of your kindness and friendship. I could never thank you both enough.

Anna and Clare, you two are simply wonderful. There is no possible way I could have done this without your expertise (or your patience!) Also, thank you Trina for your lovely styling, Geoff for the fabulous photography, and Mark for the colorful design.

And lastly, please allow me to indulge and give a shout out to my lurcher Rookie and my greyhound Rumer, for no other reason than the fact that I love them and they supply me with never-ending, unconditional love!